Th

DYSLEXIA

Help Handbook

For Parents

**Your Guide to Overcoming
Dyslexia Including Tools You
Can Use for Learning
Empowerment**

By Sandra K. Cook,
M.S. Instructional Design

DEDICATION

This book is dedicated to my two wonderful sons who taught me more than I ever imagined I would learn when I became a parent. Their unique personalities, learning styles, and learning needs have carried me along a path of love and fulfillment I never dreamed possible. We had many challenges and frustrations along the way, but our bonds have grown closer through compassionate schooling at home. My guys have made me a better, stronger person and they have revealed a strength of character, deepness of love, and driven sense of purpose within me which was not evident before our battle with dyslexia and ADHD issues. In traveling the road to overcoming dyslexia together, I have been blessed and am eternally thankful for my boys. I am immensely proud of the young men they have become.

CONTENTS

ACKNOWLEDGMENTS

Many thanks to Renee Herman for consulting with me by phone to help me better understand how to help a child with severe dyslexia learn to read. She also taught me what is essential to do, and to avoid, in providing an instructional program to overcome dyslexia.

I'd also like to thank my wonderful team of editors who have helped me polish the content in the book to make it the best resource it can be for parents who are struggling to meet the needs of their Learning Abled Kids. I'd like to personally thank Venita Schlotfeldt, Karen Cavallaro, Patricia Puntin, Cindi S., and Jeannie P. for their time and attention to punctuation and grammar details that I am prone to overlooking. I pray their editing skills bring you reading that is easy and undistracted by errors.

INTRODUCTION

Are you confused, overwhelmed, or emotional as you try to figure out how to help your child overcome dyslexia? Does your child need glasses? Color overlays? Special text fonts? Focal point training? Vision therapy? A special reading program?

Have school personnel dismissed your concerns about your child's reading struggles or told you they don't "recognize" dyslexia? Are they dragging their feet when it's clear your child needs help with reading? Have they gone as far as telling you to lower your expectations for your child's educational outcomes?

As the mom of a child with severe dyslexia, I've been there and dealt with all of the above, and even had one of our school administrators snap at me, "You just need to lower your expectations!" It's difficult to sort out the rhetoric from schools and the hype in the dyslexia solutions marketplace, so you can help your child become academically successful.

WELCOME TO RELIEF from the confusion. As an Instructional Designer, I have been able to sort out conditions, solutions, and the marketplace while helping my son. He has now graduated from college, Magna Cum Laude, and I'm confident I can help you sort things out on behalf of your child too.

Dyslexia seems to be a perplexing learning disability to overcome, but I think that is primarily because we have so many solutions thrown at us as possible solutions to "dyslexia." Every marketer and his brother wants to sell you his solution as **_the_** solution to your child's reading problem.

Confusion is increased when public school personnel declare, "We don't diagnose dyslexia," as a way of dismissing your questions about your child's struggles with learning to read. This all adds up to a recipe for frustration and failure when you can't find the right help for your child.

Over the past decade of trying to help parents sort it all out, I have figured out how to help my own sons. I've also helped countless other parents through my support group and website, LearningAbledKids.com.

I believe the confusion stems from marketers latching onto the definition of the word dyslexia and hyping their products as **_the_** solution to your child's "dyslexia." In their marketing copy, they fail to explain that their use of the word dyslexia is based upon the word's definition instead of the diagnosis of the specific learning disability called dyslexia.

Some marketers fail to tell you their products won't work for children who have the neurological, specific learning disability (SLD), called dyslexia, which is rooted in a child's lack of phonemic awareness. Marketers muddy the market by using the broad definition of the word "dyslexia" as a label over every diagnosable kind of reading difficulty.

What's the difference between the definition of the word dyslexia and a diagnosis of dyslexia?

The definition of the word dyslexia is "difficulty with reading." The prefix "dys" means something doesn't function properly and "lexia" is based in the Greek root for "word." When put together, the definition of the word dyslexia is "difficulty with words." Thus, people commonly think "dyslexia" encompasses all difficulty with reading.

All reading difficulties could be called "dyslexia" if you only consider this definition. However, if you consider difficulties with reading by each individual diagnosis, there are a large number of reading problems that are not due to diagnosable dyslexia, or what I refer to as "true dyslexia." A child can have ocular motor deficiencies, scotopic sensitivity, visual-perception difficulties, etc., all of which cause difficulty with reading, but do not fit into the diagnosis of dyslexia.

As far as diagnoses go, there is a specific learning disability (SLD) that is diagnosed as "dyslexia." This SLD is neurological in origin, involves a lack of phonemic awareness, and may have other accompanying neurological difficulties with memory, processing speed, executive functions, etc. This neurological SLD is called dyslexia, and it cannot be cured with glasses, fonts, or other "products."

Thus, from this point forward, when I use the term "dyslexia," I will be referring to this neurologically-based reading difficulty which stems from a lack of phonemic awareness and deficits in other neurological processes which is clinically diagnosed by a neuropsychologist or psychologist, and called "dyslexia" or "specific learning disability in reading" in the diagnosis.

I will talk about solutions to other reading problems caused by other diagnosable conditions, but I will call each of those conditions by their correct, diagnosable names so that you can separate true dyslexia (the SLD) from other conditions which cause difficulty with reading.

The key to finding the proper solution(s) for your child is for you to be aware of different conditions that cause reading problems. You need to be aware that marketers are all trying to get you to buy their product as a cure for your child's reading struggles, but the specific product may or may not be the proper solution for your child. Additionally, your child may have multiple conditions impacting his reading, so it is well worth exploring the wider variety of reading problems and possible solutions.

I hope this book will help you figure out precisely what your individual child may need in the way of evaluations and/or solutions to his reading difficulties. There is no guaranty this book contains the answer to your child's struggles, but I do hope it will help you sort through marketed solutions for dyslexia based upon the definition of the word. I hope the book will help enough to bring your child to a better outcome academically.

A number of kids will indeed be "cured" of reading difficulties with simple products like glasses or special fonts because they do not have true, diagnosable dyslexia. It's worth noting: if your child has the specific, neurological learning disability called dyslexia, then special glasses, special types of print, exercises of various types, etc. may be of some benefit if he has an overlapping condition, but the product alone will not provide an instant cure.

If your child has the clinically diagnosed, neurological, specific learning disability called dyslexia, he will not be magically cured by any simple, product-based solutions alone. Your child will need a reading remediation program specifically created to teach reading skills to children with phonological awareness deficits and true dyslexia.

In the first two chapters of this book, we'll examine the different types of products sold as solutions for reading difficulties based upon the definition of the word "dyslexia." The remainder of the book will discuss how you can help your child overcome the neurologically-based SLD called dyslexia. My assumption will be that your child has been diagnosed with deficits in phonological awareness, phonological memory/recall, and/or other neurological difficulties as I make instructional recommendations.

Your child may also have other physical or neurological conditions that make learning to read difficult, so you will want to consider all of the other possibilities too. The key is to read and consider each option as it relates to your individual child's reading difficulties. Use the information that seems to apply to your child and ignore whatever seems totally unrelated to your child.

CAUTION: I cannot possibly diagnose your child's specific disabilities or individual learning needs through this book. I'm not a neuropsychologist, therapist, or any other professional who can diagnose any disability in your child.

Please consult with qualified professionals in seeking a qualified diagnosis for your child in regard to each disability discussed. Only a qualified evaluator can determine whether your child needs the specific solutions discussed in this book, so please seek help when trying to pinpoint the specific needs of your child.

Who Am I and What Do I Know?

I am Sandy Cook, an Instructional Designer with training in Orton-Gillingham methods for overcoming dyslexia who has walked this road with my own boys. I'm the creator and founder of Learning Abled Kids, L.L.C. I have a support group with more than 1600 parent-members who are homeschooling to help their children overcome learning challenges and I've run the support group for more than a decade.

I've studied Universal Design for Learning (UDL) to enable children of widely varying abilities to learn, and I'm the author of *Overcome Your Fear of Homeschooling*. I've been there and done that—I taught my child with severe dyslexia how to read at home and problem-solved to provide additional solutions my son needed in order to be equipped to read well.

My instructional design background has taught me to evaluate each learner as an individual, to assess each individual child's needs, and to help seek out solutions for meeting that child's needs. I know from experience, that a carefully selected and applied solution can create a fabulous educational outcome.

This book is my heartfelt outreach to help a broader number of parents (you) find solutions to help their (your) individual child. The battle against low expectations for children with learning disabilities tugs at my very soul. There is such a great loss of human potential when our beloved children aren't given the solutions they need to help them succeed educationally.

I hope you'll to find the informational treasures needed, so you can enable your child to succeed. My prayer is that you can create a fabulous outcome for your child just like I was able to provide for my boys.

A Little Bit About Our Story

I was able to teach my sons how to read even though my older son has severe dyslexia and I'd never taught before. This may not sound like a magnificent task, but is more impressive if I tell you my older son was in public school for five years, was in a special reading program each day, and had not learned to read even while receiving specialized reading instruction from a "highly qualified" reading teacher every day at school.

In addition, we had hired a tutor to work with our son once or twice per week, but none of the help he received from others equaled any meaningful progress in his ability to read. After five years in school, independent testing showed my son was still reading on a kindergarten level—that means he was not really reading at all.

When my son was nearing the end of fourth grade, we had an Individual Education Plan (IEP) meeting where my husband and I expressed concern about our son's total lack of meaningful educational progress. One of the administrators at our school told my husband and me it was unlikely our son would "ever learn to read well." She said we just needed to lower our expectations. She even told us our son was "not college material" even though he was only in fourth grade. She had clearly given up on our son, and she advocated for us to give up on our son too!

Yes—according to the school—give up now because your child will probably never read... REALLY??

NEVER give up on your child! I began praying a lot for insight and solutions. Our good news: the Lord provides. Through diligent research and proper educational provisioning, my diligence in meeting my son's educational needs paid off handsomely.

My husband and I were not willing to allow our son to grow up illiterate, nor did we want his career options to be limited by his inability to read. Therefore, we decided we had to intervene if our son was going to go to college and pursue his dream career.

I enrolled in a two week Orton-Gillingham training course, which I completed during the summer. Then we pulled both of our sons out of public school and I taught them how to read at home.

My older son went from a kindergarten reading level to a sixth-grade equivalent reading level in our first year of homeschooling. During our second year of providing home instruction, my son's reading skills advanced to a 10th grade equivalent, and the third year he was able to achieve a 13+ grade equivalent in reading. He was able to read grade level materials as well as a college student. As icing on our cake, my son has now graduated from college, earning his Bachelor of Science Degree Magna Cum Laude!

Lest you think our journey was a walk in the park, easy and beautiful, I have to be honest and tell you that working with your child to overcome true dyslexia at home is not an endeavor for the tired, disorganized, hot-tempered, screaming banshee woman. Up front, you must realize that a child with true dyslexia has an extremely difficult time remembering specific sound-symbol relations for reading and a lot of direct instruction must be provided.

Whether you homeschool or not, whether you teach your child yourself or hire someone else to do the job, if your child has diagnosable dyslexia, then your patience will be exercised and must prevail. It is a time-consuming task to teach a child with true dyslexia how to read, but it is not a complicated task nor rocket science.

I will share with you all I know. I will also address other factors which may affect your child's ability to read—factors which are not dyslexia at all, but which people sometimes think are part of a dyslexia diagnosis.

You'll want to be sure you address your child's precise needs. Don't assume your child has true, diagnosable dyslexia when he may have other conditions, or multiple conditions, that are affecting his ability to read.

If you haven't had an evaluation of your child to determine if he has true dyslexia or other specific learning disabilities, you would benefit from seeking an evaluation. It's a lot of work to undertake teaching a child with true dyslexia how to read and you don't want to spend hours upon hours working with your child if it is the wrong solution to your child's reading difficulties.

When we undertook remediation of our son's dyslexia at home, I started with a comprehensive neuropsychological evaluation and analyzed my son's needs from there. The tools I chose were the best on the market at that time, they were great tools, and they are still available. You can use the same tools if you want established, tried and true programs.

There are also many new programs and apps on the market which can help you in teaching your child. I've researched to find viable options which are available today. Whenever possible, I've tried to make sure the products I list have some sort of research-proven basis for their effectiveness.

As you know, the market changes quickly, so there may be a better solution available by the time you read this book.

Therefore, throughout the book, when I make recommendations, feel free to search for or choose to use similar tools or products. Your main goal will be to choose similar products which have the necessary features. It will help a lot if you and your child like the product you choose.

There are a large number of products and programs available which help teach children to read, but the vast majority of these products are geared toward children who do not have dyslexia. Therefore, when searching for alternate solutions to those listed in this book, be sure to pay attention to the essential instructional features and methods needed for overcoming true dyslexia.

The last thing you want to do is waste your time or money on a product which will not work well for your child. Therefore, as I mention specific instructional methods or processes, you will want to keep them in mind so you can verify the program you choose will be worthwhile and effective for your child.

A separate consideration for helping your child overcome dyslexia at home is the amount and quality of time you have available to work one-on-one with your child. Homeschooling is not required, but it sure makes it easier to meet the needs of your child if you can homeschool—even if it is just for two or three years.

Realizing it isn't feasible for everyone to homeschool, I will differentiate different ways to work with your child as well as make recommendations for the best times to work with your child if he remains in a traditional school. School issues and lengthy homework situations make it more difficult to overcome dyslexia, but you can improve your child's educational outcomes by helping your child as much as possible at home.

In our case, I was spending so much time dealing with educational issues and homework, that I began saying, "I could have homeschooled by now!" Dealing with the school's poor educational provisioning and my son's lack of educational progress was extremely time-consuming.

We were panic-stricken that our son would be entering middle school still unable to read, so we decided we would homeschool for three years, or until my son was able to read. I had no intention of homeschooling for the remainder of my boy's K-12 years.

Homeschooling was a blessing because we were able to focus on reading skills for a couple of hours every day and we were still able to finish all of our schoolwork by mid-afternoon. We had no homework. It was such a relief and less stressful for all of us to finish the school day around 2:00 or 3:00 pm.

This does not mean that you must homeschool, but if you can, homeschooling allows you to transform your child into a proficient reader more quickly. If you can only homeschool for one or two academic years, those years can create a transformation in the life of your child if you are focused and work diligently.

If you can't homeschool at all, you will want to work intensely with your child each summer, and during holiday breaks. On a weekly basis during the school year, you can provide regular reading instruction each weekend, accompanied by before-bed practice with a computer program on a nightly basis, until your child can read.

I do not recommend trying to work with your child on remedial reading instruction after a long day at a traditional school. It is very difficult for a child with dyslexia to go to school, do what is extremely difficult for him all day long, and then come home and work on remedial reading. I've never known a child with dyslexia to come home from school ready and eager to work on reading skills; that scenario just does not happen.

Why is it so difficult to work with your child on reading after a long day at school? Your child is mentally fatigued at the end of the school day. He is likely to be short-tempered and frustrated. His fatigued mind is unlikely to retain additional instruction, and the homework he has to complete will tax any measure of patience he may have left.

Additionally, if you have been working at a job all day long, you will also be tired and prone to being impatient when your child is irritable. Therefore, I do not recommend trying to work with your child at the end of a typical school day. Doing so will drive you and your child to tears faster than you can flash glares of anger at one another.

Your implementation of remedial programs will vary depending upon whether you are teaching your child as a tutor or as a homeschool teacher. Therefore, as we talk about programs and solutions, I'll give you hints and tips for working with your child differentiated by whether your child is in a traditional school or homeschooled.

With this little introduction out of the way, let us embark on the journey to figure out exactly what your child needs and how to meet his individual reading needs.

Are you ready? Let's go…

SORTING IT ALL OUT

Before we dive into the specifics for remediation of true dyslexia, let's talk a bit further about what dyslexia is and what it is not. I'll also share considerations you may need to address in order to teach your child to read even if she only has dyslexia by definition and not by diagnosis.

It is extremely important to distinguish the difference between issues or problems with reading which are not the learning disability called dyslexia. As we discussed in the Introduction, people use the definition of dyslexia as if it were a diagnosis of dyslexia, and the definition is quite different from the diagnosis of the learning disability called dyslexia.

There is a critical difference between what is required to address a child's developmental vision issues, scotopic sensitivity, visual-perception, or speech language issues versus what is required to remediate true dyslexia. So let us begin by defining specifically what diagnosable dyslexia is and what it is not.

Dyslexia, as diagnosed by a psychologist or neuropsychologist, is a neurological, cognitive, and specific learning disability. A child with true dyslexia has difficulty with phonemic awareness as the hallmark characteristic of his reading difficulties. In other words, if your child does not have deficits in phonemic awareness, then he probably has a reading disability other than true dyslexia.

Although definitions vary from one neurologically-based profession to another, phonemic awareness deficiencies are common across definitions for diagnosable dyslexia. As a disability, dyslexia often has additional difficulties with processing speed, executive functions, and/or working memory, which we'll discuss further in the next chapter as we discuss forms of diagnosable dyslexia.

The National Institute of Neurological Disorders and Stroke says, "Although the disorder varies from person to person, common characteristics among people with dyslexia are *difficulty with phonological processing* (the manipulation of sounds), spelling, and/or rapid visual-verbal responding" (National Institute of Neurological Disorders and Stroke, 2013).

The International Dyslexia Association says, "Dyslexia is a specific learning disability that is <u>neurological in origin</u>. It is characterized by difficulties with accurate and/or fluent word recognition and by poor spelling and decoding abilities. These difficulties typically result from *a deficit in the phonological component* of language that is often unexpected in relation to other cognitive abilities and the provision of effective classroom instruction" (International Dyslexia Association, 2013).

As you can see from the definitions of diagnosable dyslexia, it is not a vision-based problem. True dyslexia will not be cured by fabulous fonts, great glasses, or eye exercises. Each of these treatments may help children who have difficulty with reading, but they will not cure diagnosable dyslexia which is a neurologically-based specific learning disability (SLD).

There are many conditions which cause difficulty with reading, but contrary to popular opinion, they are not all clinically lumped together as one condition called "dyslexia." However, that doesn't mean we can ignore these other conditions that cause difficulty with reading. It is important for you to know these different conditions which cause difficulty with reading, so you can seek the appropriate interventions for your child.

Treatments vary significantly for each of the conditions that cause difficulty with reading. Since you are seeking to obtain the correct treatment for your child's specific condition, I'll spend a lot of time clarifying conditions and options in this and the next chapter.

For now, let's see if we can help you clarify the distinctions between products marketed as cures for "dyslexia" (by definition, but not by diagnosis). The remainder of this chapter discusses conditions which affect a child's ability to read, but which are not the specific learning disability called dyslexia. Your child may have both non-SLD based reading disabilities and diagnosable dyslexia, so it will be important for you to read through all of the possibilities in order to determine the root cause(s) of your individual child's reading difficulties.

To be a wise consumer, always ask yourself, "Is this marketer talking about the diagnosable, neurological learning disability called "dyslexia," or is he using the word "dyslexia" based upon the definition of the word? If the marketer is using the definition of dyslexia, which reading problem is this product or service actually designed to solve?"

Ask yourself these critical questions before you consider purchasing various solutions. To make things even more difficult, your child may have one, two, or maybe all of the various conditions that cause reading struggles. Therefore, you'll have to have your child evaluated to determine whether your child has diagnosable dyslexia or some other condition that is causing his difficulty with reading in order to know which types of solutions to seek.

Given that multiple conditions may be interfering with

your child's ability to read, let's spend a little time talking about what you can do to determine which of these non-SLD problems your child may have and how you can tackle them. There are some inexpensive ways to assess your child in a general sense, but having a paid professional accurately diagnose your child will be the most effective way to determine your child's needs.

I'm sharing the information in this chapter to minimize the amount of information hunting you must undertake. However, be aware: I am not a doctor and the information I share here is only for informational purposes. The information I'll share with you is from my instructional design perspective, from the past decade of helping countless families figure out how to meet their child's individual needs, and from hours upon hours of reading research.

I know you want to move forward with meeting your child's needs, but ***you must seek a professional evaluation and diagnosis for any condition you think your child may have in order to properly and accurately meet your child's educational needs. You alone are 100% responsible for seeking a proper diagnosis for your child.***

You are responsible for making sure you obtain a diagnosis from a qualified professional. Let me reiterate, the information I share here is informative in nature and is not intended to be used to diagnose your child. Only a qualified professional can adequately and accurately diagnose your child.

The information I share here is "screening" in nature. In other words, the resources I point you to are intended to help you decide whether you need to seek a professional evaluation or diagnosis for your child. No screening is totally accurate. Therefore, it is essential you seek a professional evaluation for any condition you suspect your child may have to ensure you are addressing the correct learning problem for your child.

When determining if your child should be

professionally evaluated for any of the listed conditions, whether or not your child also has true dyslexia, it is helpful to address any physical barriers to reading your child has before diving into a dyslexia-based reading program.

If your child cannot process the instruction you are providing due to scotopic sensitivity, ocular motor issues, visual-perception issues, or auditory processing issues, then the reading instruction you provide is likely to create frustration and your child's progress will be inhibited. You can minimize your child's frustration and unnecessary repetition by addressing underlying physical conditions first.

For each of the non-dyslexia conditions mentioned here, I will provide information about informal screening, resources for finding a professional to assess your child, and I'll suggest some tools and methods for helping your child. I will also list the conditions in the order of easiest to hardest to overcome, so you can address the easy issues first. We'll talk about diagnosed dyslexia in the next chapter, but let's first talk about the other conditions which people often lump together with dyslexia based upon the definition of the word.

Scotopic Sensitivity or Irlen Syndrome

Colored glasses, color overlays, and pastel papers are advertised or sold as solutions for "dyslexia" by various vendors. The advertising is based upon the definition of the word dyslexia, not a dyslexia diagnosis.

When people use colored overlays or colored glasses to treat reading difficulties, they are actually treating scotopic sensitivity, which is also sometimes called the "Irlen Syndrome," named after Helen Irlen, who discovered that colored glasses, overlays, or pastel papers can immediately enable some children to read.

Scotopic sensitivity is a light-spectrum sensitivity where certain portions of the light spectrum can make it difficult for an individual to focus on words appearing on white paper or white boards. The high contrast of black text on white paper is simply more glaring and difficult to some people than it is to others.

Children with Scotopic Sensitivity sometimes complain of their eyes being tired, they may develop headaches while trying to read, often prefer dim lighting, and prefer low-glare paper for reading. Simple solutions include using a low-glare green or black chalkboard, blue boards instead of whiteboards, and other colorful solutions.

Scotopic Sensitivity (SS) or the Irlen Syndrome is the easiest non-dyslexia reading difficulty to overcome. As a very first step in determining whether this syndrome may be a factor in your child's reading difficulties, I'd recommend using the "Self Test" tool on the Irlen Institute website at http://irlen.com/get-tested/. Some of the self-test items can ALSO be evident in a child with true dyslexia or other reading disabilities, so please don't make the mistake of thinking the symptoms assessed are definitive evidence of the presence of Scotopic Sensitivity or that they indicate your child does not have another problem interfering with his ability to read.

Most notably, if your child becomes fatigued while reading or finds it difficult to read for long periods, this can indicate Scotopic Sensitivity, dyslexia, ocular motor difficulties, all of the above, or something else. Fatigue when reading is one of the most common symptoms for any child with learning difficulties, so it isn't really a reliable indicator of any specific condition or a strong indicator of SS.

Having red, watery eyes or needing to use your finger to keep your place can be indicative of ocular motor deficits. Similarly, re-reading lines, needing frequent breaks, or being easily distracted are symptoms that are also evident with attention deficit disorder, visual perception difficulties, or ocular motor deficiencies, so these indicators are not definitive indications of Scotopic Sensitivity. Your child may have Scotopic Sensitivity (SS), but he may have another condition instead of or in addition to SS.

Thus, the key to determining whether your child may have Scotopic Sensitivity is to realize that having a majority of the symptoms together is a better indicator of having SS than some of the symptoms. If your child has a significant level of physical distress with reading, it is likely your child has Scotopic Sensitivity, visual processing deficits, or ocular motor deficiencies. Look for evidence that may sway you one way or the other in determining which route to pursue first. In the interest of thoroughness, you may want to pursue each of the routes of evaluation.

If your child's self-screening leads you to believe your child may have SS, you will want to understand Scotopic Sensitivity better. There are three books I'd recommend. You don't have to read all of them, but if you think your child may have Scotopic Sensitivity, then you'll want to read at least one of the books.

The first book is called, *Reading by the Colors* by Helen Irlen. You will notice the author is the founder of the Irlen Institute and she is the one who studied and discovered the syndrome known as the Irlen Syndrome involving Scotopic Sensitivity. As the founder, she is the definitive expert on the topic, and you will learn a great deal about the syndrome from her book.

Helen Irlen also has a book called, *The Irlen Revolution: A Guide to Changing Your Perception and Your Life*, which is geared more toward correcting Visual-perception issues than light spectrum issues. You'll notice the book description and comments by reviewers hail this as a miracle solution for "dyslexia." Just be keenly aware— they are using the definition of the word dyslexia, and not referring to the diagnosable learning disability which stems from a lack of phonemic awareness.

Glasses and color overlays in no way correct deficits in phonemic awareness. Glasses and color overlays correct SS and Irlen Syndrome, but they will not correct neurologically-based true dyslexia. This distinction between the different conditions which cause difficulty with reading cannot be stressed strongly enough to you.

You absolutely must determine the root of your child's individual problem(s) and address his specific disabilities. Do not eagerly seek miracle cures for "dyslexia" without knowing the distinct differences between conditions which cause difficulty with reading. You are likely to waste your time and money on solutions that don't address the precise problem your child has if you do not carefully assess and address the specific causes of your child's reading difficulties.

If you are skeptical about receiving diagnostic help from someone who's goal is to sell you the solution, you may prefer getting information from someone who understands the syndrome, but who does not sell a solution. If so, you may prefer to read Rhonda Stone's book, *The Light Barrier: A Color Solution to Your Child's Light-based Reading Difficulties.* Mrs. Stone is a journalist whose children have scotopic sensitivity, so she has researched the topic thoroughly and reports on it through her book. You might find her experience more relatable as a mom.

As a light spectrum sensitivity, Scotopic Sensitivity can also cause visual distortion. The sensitivities and distortion are corrected by using special glasses, color overlays, low-glare or colored papers, traditional chalkboards and other low-tech solutions. The remedies are easy to purchase and put to use, so if your child has SS, you should be able to correct the problem relatively quickly and inexpensively.

If you'd like your child formally assessed for Scotopic Sensitivity, visit the Irlen Institute at http:/irlen.com/ and use their Test Center Locator to find the closest evaluator near you. Additional information and resources are provided on the Irlen website which will help you understand scotopic sensitivity better. Taking the time to watch their video clips is worthwhile.

While having your child professionally evaluated is the only conclusive way to obtain a diagnosis, many parents have opted to purchase color overlays from a supplier of office products or they've tried various pastel paper colors for worksheets to see if these aids improve their child's symptoms.

If your child is diagnosed with SS, you can buy a set of Irlen Color overlays on Amazon to see if they help your child. See: http://www.amazon.com/IRLEN-Colored-Overlays-Reading-Sample/dp/B003LNMHTU/).

When you print worksheets, you can print them on pastel colored paper and see if your child has an easier time using the colored worksheets.

Although using overlays and colored paper won't give you a clear indicator of whether your child suffers from S.S., it is an easy way to see if the colors help your child. If they do, then you should pursue a full evaluation.

If your child has SS, then specially colored glasses can correct the light spectrum no matter what type of written material your child is reading. If your child needs these colored glasses, they can seem like a miracle cure indeed!

Ocular Motor Deficiencies

Similar to Scotopic Sensitivity, people often suggest a child with "dyslexia" should have vision therapy, but vision therapy does not correct true dyslexia. Vision therapy treats developmental eye deficiencies, also known as "ocular motor deficits."

Ocular motor difficulties are caused by developmental issues in the muscles used for moving your eyeballs. When a child cannot smoothly sweep his eyes from side-to-side, it is difficult for him to focus on the words as he tries to read. Children may have rapid eye movements, trembling in their muscles, or other muscular or neurological conditions that make it difficult for them to focus on individual words, much less to move their eyes smoothly across the text.

Children with ocular motor deficits often complain about their eyes hurting, about words jumping around on the page, and often lose their place while reading. They may skip words or entire lines of text while reading because their eyes have not tracked straight across a line of text.

If your child has complaints about his eyes hurting while reading, you'll want to consider ocular motor deficiencies as a possible issue. Ocular motor deficiencies or developmental vision deficits cause many of the same symptoms as scotopic sensitivity or Irlen Syndrome. You can use the self-test on the Irlen Institute Website to determine if your child has a significant number of the eye-strain related indicators and/or the visual tracking indicators like losing his place on a page or experiencing words "jumping around" on a page.

It is my experience that children with ocular motor deficits experience more abrupt "jumping" of words on the page and more significant shifts in their visual tracking, whereas those with SS are more likely to experience distortion. The differences between the two vision-related issues is very difficult for a parent to discern, so you are likely to need an evaluation from a developmental optometrist to determine if your child has any ocular motor deficiencies.

To find a good developmental optometrist, visit the College of Optometrists in Vision Development at: http://www.covd.org/ and use their zip code tool to find a trained doctor near you.

Be aware: developmental vision issues are not the same as visual acuity issues. Your child can have 20/20 vision and still have ocular motor issues. 20/20 vision means your child can see objects clearly. However your child's eye muscles may not be fully developed, may be weak, and not well-controlled.

If your child has ocular motor issues then his eyes may

quiver when moving, may move in a jerky way, may not have the full range of motion, etc. Developmental Optometrists are specially trained to assess a child's eye movement as a separate issue from the child's ability to see things clearly.

If your child has developmental vision issues, either with smooth eye movements or adequate near-far focusing, then he will probably require vision therapy. For a long time, people didn't realize how beneficial vision therapy can be, but a lot of research has been undertaken and vision therapy is shown to be of significant benefit to kids who need it. You can read more about vision therapy research at: http://www.covd.org/?page=Research&hhSearchTerms=research.

Vision therapy treatments vary with the child's specific needs and with individual doctors. Some doctors prefer to be hands-on with the therapy, whereas others act as therapy coaches who will teach you the exercises and let you work with your child at home. Some doctors use computer programs and 3D glasses with prescribed treatment plans.

Working with your child at home is preferable if you have a busy schedule or the doctor is a distance from your home. The variations from one doctor to another can be significant, so you will want to inquire about how the doctor prefers to handle therapy while choosing your vision therapy doctor.

Most often a doctor will create a treatment plan and will teach you how to work with your child on his eye exercises. You will have monthly or bi-monthly sessions with your developmental optometrists to check your child's progress and to assess for needed changes to the therapy regimen.

If your child requires vision therapy, you and your child must be committed to the process of performing the required exercises daily. Diligence in performing the exercises is the primary difference between successful vision therapy and therapy that drags on for years or doesn't seem to work at all. By making your child's vision therapy a daily priority, you can shorten the amount of time it takes to move your child from experiencing eye strain to reading comfortably.

When my son had vision therapy with a developmental optometrist, he prescribed a "Home Vision Therapy" program that my son used with a pair of 3-D glasses and our home computer. The program was very beneficial and enabled my son to shorten the number of months he had to endure vision therapy.

Once every six weeks we returned to the optometrist for re-evaluation and for the optometrist to adjust the settings in the computer program. We found using this type of program made it easy for us to comply with the required therapy regimen prescribed by our COVD-qualified doctor.

There are several books about vision therapy on Amazon if you search for "vision therapy," along with a couple of home-based vision therapy programs. The program my son used, as overseen by our doctor, was Home Vision Therapy at http://www.homevisiontherapy.com/.

You will notice there is a "Contact Doctors" option on the Home Vision Therapy website, which you can use to find a doctor that can help you use this specific home vision therapy system. To learn more about ocular motor deficiencies and vision therapy, visit the College of Optometrists in Vision Development at: http://www.covd.org/.

Visual-Perception Difficulties

Similarly, people sometimes think visual-perceptual difficulties are at the heart of a dyslexia diagnosis, but here again, visual-perception difficulties do not specifically involve a lack of phonemic awareness. Children may be diagnosed with dyslexia without having any visual-perception difficulties.

It's important to note that some children who have visual-perception deficits or overwhelming strengths also have deficits in phonemic awareness. It is not uncommon for a child to have visual-perception issues accompanying a dyslexia diagnosis based upon a lack of phonemic awareness.

Whether a child has visual-perception difficulties, true dyslexia, or both conditions, we must distinguish visual-perception and true dyslexia as distinctly different disabilities for your remediation purposes.

If a child has visual-perception difficulties, the visual-perception issues need to be treated in a different way than dyslexia-based phonemic awareness deficits. Visual-perception issues require brain-training and/or therapies. Sometimes a child with visual-perception difficulties finds a dramatic improvement in his ability to read when specialized fonts are used for text. The new "Dyslexia Font" is one of the simplest tools that aids children who have difficulty with reading due to visual-perception problems

Children with visual-perception deficits may also have difficulty with eye-hand coordination and fine motor skills required for neat handwriting. Visual-perception problems are often at the heart of the letter reversals commonly seen when children have significant difficulty with reading. I believe these reversals occur most often when a child has a strong ability to view objects three dimensionally in their minds, so that the orientation of similar letters like p, d, b, and q, u and n, m and w, all become the same object in three-dimensional space.

Visual-perception difficulties are more difficult to treat than scotopic sensitivity or ocular motor deficiencies. They are also more difficult to diagnose. Issues with visual-perceptual abilities are typically assessed during a comprehensive neuro-psychological evaluation. Two common evaluation instruments used to test for visual perceptual deficiencies are the Test of Visual Perceptual Skills (TVPS) and the Developmental Test of Visual Perception (DTVP).

If your child has had a comprehensive evaluation, you may want to check the evaluation report to see if the TVPS or DTVP were administered, or if some other test of visual-perception was used. If you suspect your child may have visual-perception difficulties, you may want to inquire about having your neuropsychologist test your child specifically for visual-perception. Look for either very high or very low scores in this area to determine if visual perception training may be needed.

It's important to note, visual/perceptual issues are often present in children who have difficulty with reading, and visual/perceptual problems co-exist with phonemic awareness issues in some percentage of the population. I can't find any precise research studies to determine the frequency with which children who have true dyslexia also have visual/perceptual difficulties, but in my personal experience there is a noteworthy overlap.

Thus, if your child has visual-perception issues, you may still need to have him assessed for phonemic awareness deficits. A comprehensive evaluation should include tests for both visual-perception and phonemic awareness difficulties, but you can ask your evaluator just to be sure both areas will be assessed.

If your child has visual-perception deficits, you'll want to pursue visual-perception training for your child. There are several methods used for overcoming visual-perception difficulties, but there is no single, perfect solution that meets every child's needs. What works for one child may not work for another, so this is one area of remediation where you may have to experiment to see what works for your child.

Let's talk about a few different methods for helping a child overcome visual-perception deficits:

1) The Irlen Syndrome treatments can help with some forms of visual-perception issues. Thus, if your child may benefit from Irlen Syndrome treatments and you haven't

already ruled out the Irlen Syndrome, you may want to contact the Irlen Institute to see if your child's visual-perception problems can be corrected through their products.

2) The most notable "at home" resource I know that addresses visual-perception issues is *The Gift of Dyslexia.* This book and the "Davis Method" seeks to help children overcome difficulties with reading primarily by teaching them to maintain a "focal point."

The Gift of Dyslexia also provides instruction for working with clay and letters to help solidify the phonemes and alphabetic representations in their proper orientations, so there is a component in the book that also addresses phonemic awareness. The "Davis Method" is focused on helping with visual perceptual issues as heavily as, if not more so than teaching the phonemes, so if your child has significant phonemic awareness deficits, he may need intense remediation for phonemic awareness from a program specifically designed to overcome those deficits, whether or not he also needs visual-perception training.

Although the Davis "focal point" methodology is not a traditional treatment method for true dyslexia, it can be of benefit to children with visual-perception issues. Given the book is inexpensive and the methodology is easy to provide, it could be worth trying to see if the program will help your child.

3) If you'd like a free Visual-perception program online, check out http://www.eyecanlearn.com/. The exercises are reminiscent of those used in computer-based ocular motor training, therefore I feel the program might help strengthen visual processing, but this is not a proven program. It is recommended as a supplemental training tool.

4) A good program, which we used, is Lexia's "Cross-Trainer: Visual-Spatial." The program exercises visual

memory, mental rotation, visual tracking, spatial orientation, visualization, and multi-perspective coordination. The program can be found at: http://www.literacyandmaths.co.nz/cross-trainer.html.

We used the Cross Trainer program along with my son's Vision Therapy to help with his letter reversals and visual-perception. The combined methodology was effective for my son, but I don't know to what degree the Cross Trainer programs will help your child.

5) The Visual Perception Laboratory researches eye movements, eye tracking, and visual-perception as aspects of overall perception. If your child has ocular motor issues, Irlen Syndrome, or visual-perception issues, you may want to visit the Visual Perception Laboratory at Rochester Institute of Technology: http:/www.cis.rit.edu/vpl/ to learn more about each of these pieces of the vision-based reading puzzle.

6) There is a so-called "Dyslexia Font" that helps children with visual-perception difficulties when reading. As with other products, the "Dyslexia Font" uses the word based upon the definition and not upon the diagnosis of the specific learning disability. The font won't cure the neurological learning disability called dyslexia, but the font can be like a magic solution to reading difficulties stemming from visual-perception problems.

The Dyslexia Font has heavier lines at the bottom to help the child perceive the proper orientation of the letters. The font also has specialized spacing that makes each word easier to perceive.

This concept of using a special font to help a child with visual-perception based reading difficulties is fairly new, so there aren't many resources available yet. If your child has visual-perception problems, search for print materials using the "Dyslexia Font" and see what you can find.

You may need a combination of programs or products to address your child's visual-perception difficulties. Improving visual-perception can help make reading a lot easier from the standpoint of your child's ability to properly perceive the words on the paper.

You may want to search for additional programs and resources for improving visual/perceptual issues. Because this area is difficult to remediate, there are fewer readily available solutions for the home market, but you can probably find providers in your area that can help with visual/perception training.

Auditory Processing Disorder (APD or CAPD)

Auditory Processing Disorders (APD) often cause reading difficulties. APD (Auditory Processing Disorder) or CAPD (Central Auditory Processing Disorder) is a diagnosis widely applied to a variety of difficulties involving auditory or speech-language skills. APD is a neurologically-based learning disability that can also encompass a diagnosis of true dyslexia.

APD is a deficit in the processing of auditory information by a child's central nervous system, which makes it difficult for the child to make fine distinctions between sounds, to be able to separate sounds in noisy environments, etc. Therefore, if your child has auditory processing disorder, she is likely to have difficulty with phonemic awareness too.

APD causes more pervasive difficulty with phonemes and phonemic awareness than true dyslexia. Therefore, it requires a deeper level of speech-language based intervention than dyslexia, although APD usually requires similar, phonemic awareness-based reading instruction.

As with other disabilities, there are separate and distinct characteristics of APD which require specific treatments that are different from or added to instruction for overcoming true dyslexia. APD-based difficulties with reading are frequently remediated by using precisely the same multi-sensory, detailed, explicit, instructional programs used for remediating dyslexia.

Therefore, APD is one disability where a child can be taught to read using similar or the same methodologies as those used to teach children with dyslexia.

Similar to 20/20 vision and the presence of developmental vision issues, your child can have perfect hearing but fail to process sounds correctly. The American Speech-Language-Hearing Association has excellent information explaining Auditory Processing Disorders at: http://www.asha.org/public/hearing/disorders/understand-apd-child.htm, so I will not include the information here.

If you suspect APD, you will need to have your child specifically evaluated for APD. An ordinary hearing screening does not rule in or rule out an auditory processing disorder.

Auditory processing disorders must be diagnosed by a qualified audiologist with special training for diagnosing APD. To find a provider who is qualified to screen for an auditory processing disorder, check out ASHA's "Buyer's Guide" (http://buyersguide.asha.org/).

As mentioned in the previous chapter, Auditory Processing Disorders are often accompanied by difficulties with phonemic awareness. Therefore, if your child has APD, it is highly likely she will also have phonemic awareness deficits.

When you have a definitive APD diagnosis, if you want to help your child at home, there are some software programs designed specifically for helping with auditory processing difficulties as it relates to learning to read. Many programs designed to help a child with APD issues include phonemic awareness instruction.

If your child is struggling with reading, you will want to focus on selecting a program that integrates both auditory processing and phonemic awareness training into the program. Why?

Because having a program that works on auditory processing issues and phonemic awareness simultaneously will make the learning process more efficient for both you and your child. If phonemic awareness is not part of your child's auditory processing training and your child needs phonemic awareness instruction, you will have to provide two programs instead of one.

With the goal in mind of helping your child with both auditory processing issues and phonemic awareness, I'll share resources for you to choose from that address both issues. You may end up working with an SLP to address your child's auditory processing issues along with phonemic awareness so you may not need to address these issues at home.

If you are working on APD and/or phonemic awareness at home, the following list of programs may be helpful to you. Just be aware that some of the programs do not have phonemic awareness built into the programs, so you will need an additional phonemic awareness program if that is the case.

Linguisystems is one of the best, high quality resource companies for programs and materials to help your child at home. Linguisystems sells products used by speech-language pathologists (SLPs), but you can buy their products for home use as well. They have an extensive selection of games, kits, programs, and materials in their Language and Auditory Processing section, which can help you work with your child at home.

Super Duper Publications was created by an SLP and is similar to Linguisystems. Super Duper provides a wide variety of programs and materials for helping children with learning challenges, including auditory processing disorder. On their website, you can perform a "Topic Search" where "Auditory Processing" is a specific category you can select from their drop-down menu. There are several pages of results that come up which include games, books, computer programs, etc., you can use to help your child at home.

If you'd like to use a software program to help your child, Bungalow Software has a series of programs specifically designed for APD. One aspect I like about their software programs is that they have controlled research to document the effectiveness of their programs.

A very well-known program is "The Listening Program (TLP) by Advanced Brain Technologies." TLP is a different kind of program in that it is a program of musical orchestrations that take the listener through a cycle of accommodation, training, and integration by listening to acoustically enhanced, specially created musical selections.

The listening modules are listened to daily in a specified order, following a specific listening protocol. There is research documenting the effectiveness of the program which primarily consists of listening to music. As an at-home user, you would work with a provider who would coach you in the use of the program and help you deal with any problems or issues you may have with the program.

Since the Listening Program is musical in nature, it has no phonemic awareness component, so you would have to have an additional program to teach the phonemes to your child. If you are trying to address all of your child's needs at home, it's a good idea to consider the Earobics program (discussed later in this section) as a good addition to the Listening Program.

Lastly, but certainly not least of all, Scientific Learning provides a well-known program called Fast ForWord. If your child has both APD and phonemic awareness issues, Fast ForWord may be your best choice of all, programmatically speaking. However, the big drawback is that you cannot purchase and use the Fast ForWord program independently at home. You must go through a qualified provider who is trained in proper oversight and usage of the program.

SciLearn provides a "Find a Provider" tool on their website, which you will find in the "Parent" section of their website.

Earobics is another program that is designed to help children who have APD and phonemic awareness issues. Earobics is a great program, which we used at home, but it is not as thorough and in-depth as the Fast ForWord program. Therefore, if your child has mild difficulties, or you simply want to provide practice and review at home, then you may want to use Earobics as an inexpensive computer-based practice program.

Personally, if my child had APD, it is an area where I'd be less inclined to try to remediate the difficulties independently at home. Auditory processing difficulties are difficult to track and measure, so I think APD is one of the disabilities where working with a provider on a semi-regular basis would be beneficial for making sure your child is progressing well.

You may feel differently, but either way—I wanted to add that if you are going to work with a provider, finding one who uses the Fast ForWord program could be your most efficient route to addressing phonemic awareness-based reading difficulties combined with APD. FFW is a proven program that has a good track record.

Also, if your child has APD and you use a program with phonemic awareness instruction built into it, you might be able to bypass the upcoming section on phonemic awareness altogether. Your child will probably still need more advanced reading instruction as is required by students with true dyslexia.

If your child has phonemic awareness difficulties along with difficulties in working memory and processing, she probably has true dyslexia too, whether your school or evaluator says so or not. By following the dyslexia-based protocols for teaching a child with true dyslexia to read, you are more likely to be successful in teaching your child to read.

Other Learning Difficulties

The above list is comprised of the learning disabilities and physical deficits most often mislabeled as "dyslexia," by definition. While there are a large number of other learning disabilities that can affect reading, writing, and spelling abilities, other conditions are usually diagnosed as separate neurological or biological conditions.

For example, a child may have difficulty learning to read due to Attention Deficit Hyperactivity Disorder (ADHD). If this is the case, a parent is usually quite clear on the need to treat the ADHD as a separate and distinct condition. Although ADHD affects reading, it isn't dyslexia. Neither parents nor professionals tend to mistake ADHD for dyslexia.

Because there are so many conditions, like low vision, traumatic brain injuries, etc., which may affect a child's ability to learn to read, write, and spell well, I won't even attempt to list all of the conditions which may be affecting your child's ability to read.

However, if your child is having difficulty learning to read, it might help you to know that reading programs for children with dyslexia are multi-sensory, step-by-step, explicit, comprehensive, direct instruction programs. As such, they are often good programs for teaching children who might have a wide variety of instructional needs.

It is also essential you realize your child may have multiple conditions affecting his ability to learn how to read. For example, my older son had ocular-motor deficiencies, speech-language difficulties which affected his ability to properly sound out words, and he had severe dyslexia. We had to address the first two issues before adequate progress could be made in overcoming dyslexia.

Thus, you may have to assess your child for each of the conditions which may be affecting his ability to read, then address each condition as needed. If all of your child's needs are not being treated, you may find yourself feeling like the programs you are using "aren't working" for your child.

When programs "aren't working," the problem is not usually with the program itself, but more likely with the implementation of the program or an overlooked need your child may have. We'll talk more about implementation issues later in the book and delve into assessing your child's needs more deeply in the next chapter.

Just be aware: In order to facilitate good progress when teaching your child to read, it is essential for all areas of need to be addressed. Treating your whole child is essential for having good academic success with reading and other academics.

A Note to Providers:

It's a real problem when marketers and providers fail to separate various reading problems based upon the true root causes—whether visual, perceptual, cognitive or neurologically-based. When marketers call all reading difficulties "dyslexia," it is a disservice to everyone, especially the children who end up being subjected to any number of solutions for so-called "dyslexia" when they aren't solutions for diagnosable dyslexia.

Thus, if you are a provider of a reading solution for any condition that is not the neurological SLD called dyslexia, I implore you to label your products as solutions for the precisely diagnosed condition which it will solve. Don't use the catch all definition of the word "dyslexia" simply to target every child who has difficulty with reading. Read the two chapters, "Sorting It All Out" and "Dyslexia By Diagnosis" if you need clarification for yourself.

Pervasive misunderstandings about what dyslexia is, by definition versus diagnosis, prevents kids from receiving the appropriate therapies and programs. If you are a person who calls scotopic sensitivity, ocular motor deficiencies, visual-perception deficits, or any other condition "dyslexia" when it is not the neurologically-based specific learning disability called dyslexia, then you are contributing to the further detriment of children who are struggling to learn to read. Using dyslexia as a catch-all phrase for every condition that impacts reading makes it difficult for parents to readily find appropriate reading solutions for their children.

You can help improve outcomes by calling each specific condition by its actual name. In doing so, you will enable parents and educators to understand the different types of reading disabilities and to find specific solutions more quickly. You will become a voice for clarity rather than confusion.

DYSLEXIA BY DIAGNOSIS

As if it weren't complicated enough when people confuse the definition of dyslexia with the diagnosis of dyslexia, there are different names for different forms of dyslexia. Although the intent is to clarify the specific nature of a child's dyslexia, I think the overall effect on parents is to confuse them further!

To be clear, a diagnosis of the learning disability called dyslexia by a qualified neuropsychologist means your child has a lack of phonemic awareness. Period. Your child may have other neurological difficulties too, as the Diagnostic Manuals formerly indicated that diagnosed dyslexia is a cluster of problems. However, a lack of phonemic awareness is the defining condition that is present in all forms of diagnosed dyslexia.

In the hopes of clearing up this dyslexia soup for you, so you can figure out how to meet your child's needs, let's talk about the various forms of true dyslexia which are diagnosed. Keep in mind, for all forms of dyslexia discussed in this chapter, a lack of phonemic awareness is present.

The variations of dyslexia discussed in this chapter are simply ways of describing specific circumstances or co-existing conditions that change the severity of a child's dyslexia symptoms. The addition of co-existing conditions usually means there will be additional areas of remediation you'll need to consider. No matter what the co-existing conditions are, there are ways and means for addressing a child's individual needs.

Simple, Vanilla Dyslexia

Although dyslexia is never really simple, if your child simply lacks phonemic awareness, then his dyslexia is like vanilla ice cream instead of Rocky Road ice cream. If your child lacks phonemic awareness, has no other cognitive deficits, and has no other condition mentioned in the prior chapter, then your child should learn to read when provided with any proven dyslexia remediation program.

If you're reading this book, your child probably does not have simple, vanilla dyslexia. If your child was identified as having a lack of phonemic awareness, has been receiving detailed, direct, and comprehensive instruction in reading, but still isn't learning to read, then your child probably has additional learning barriers that haven't been identified.

If your child is in public school, had a screening for phonemic awareness, and started receiving specialized reading instruction, then you don't have a comprehensive picture of your child's learning needs. A screening for a lack of phonemic awareness will identify a problem in that area, but the screening ignores all other possible barriers to your child's learning.

If your child's school didn't perform a comprehensive evaluation, including examination of your child's memory functioning, perceptual abilities, different forms of processing information (visual, verbal, speed, etc.), attention functioning, etc., then they probably failed to identify all of your child's learning needs. If your child continues to struggle with learning to read, even when receiving direct instruction in phonemic awareness, then chances are very high that there is some other co-existing problem that is complicating your child's learning.

Sometimes other problems are identified in a comprehensive evaluation, but they are never addressed—as if they don't matter. For example, my son was known to have processing speed problems and executive function deficits, but his school only provided reading instruction. They never worked on enhancing my son's processing speed or executive functioning as part of his individual program. I don't know why schools think they can ignore everything except reading instruction when a child has multiple areas of learning difficulty that need to be strengthened.

Thus, if your child was simply identified as having a lack of phonemic awareness, but he's not learning to read, chances are high one of three problems is present:

1. There are additional neurological deficits which haven't been identified.

2. Co-existing cognitive deficits aren't being addressed.

3. Your child's reading instruction isn't being provided properly or in sufficient quantity.

We'll talk about proper program provisioning when we discuss dyslexia remediation programs in an upcoming chapter. For now, if your child has phonemic awareness deficits and isn't progressing with his individualized reading instruction, then you should consider further evaluation. You need to make sure all identified needs are being addressed, and make sure your child is receiving proper instruction.

As I said, if you're reading this book, I suspect your child doesn't have simple dyslexia with a lack of phonemic awareness with no other needs. Having a lack of phonemic awareness as an isolated cognitive deficit isn't overly difficult to overcome, but seldom is the lack of phonemic awareness an isolated problem. This fact is another reason dyslexia is so difficult to overcome, aside from the confusion over the definition versus the diagnosis of dyslexia!

Stealth Dyslexia

You may also have heard the term "stealth dyslexia" and wonder what the difference is between stealth dyslexia and simple dyslexia. For the most part, the two types of dyslexia are the same, but a child with stealth dyslexia has developed great coping skills that keep his dyslexia hidden for a longer period of time. Therefore, the difference between the two is primarily based upon the dominance of dyslexia symptoms impacting a child's learning.

Let me explain a bit further. The typical child with simple dyslexia struggles with learning to read, his spelling is often atrocious, and it is usually evident the child has a learning disability sometime during elementary school. A child with milder dyslexia may not be diagnosed until he hits upper elementary or middle school when multi-syllable words become dominant in reading and writing assignments.

A highly intelligent child with good coping skills may not show signs of dyslexia until middle school or later because he quickly learns to memorize and use coping skills that mask his dyslexia. This is frequently the case with children who are highly intelligent and have simple dyslexia.

If your child learned to read well, yet has difficulty with some aspects of classroom performance—most notably writing—then your child may need to be tested for learning disabilities. When comprehensive testing is provided, it can unexpectedly reveal underlying characteristics of dyslexia. Your child may have a lack of phonemic awareness, yet he is able to read in spite of the deficit.

When a child learns to read without major struggles, no one suspects underlying dyslexia, so it comes as a surprise to the parents and teachers to find out a child actually has dyslexia. Since the dyslexia was "hidden," it is said to be "stealth," but it was there all along.

You may wonder how any child with true dyslexia can learn to read without notable difficulty. Stealth Dyslexia occurs predominantly within the intellectually gifted population. Because the children are intelligent, creative thinkers, with strong vocabulary skills and good analytical abilities, they are able to guess the words in sentences. Guessing words based upon the topic of a sentence is a common coping skill when the child can't figure out the word through actual decoding.

Frequently, a child with stealth dyslexia will have difficulty with handwriting or written expression. He may be evaluated for dysgraphia, which is when the stealth dyslexia comes to light.

Writing difficulties are the main indicator of trouble if your child has stealth dyslexia because writing requires your child to think about what he wants to write, formulate the words in his mind, and then write or type the words. Writing words on paper is especially difficult because there are no visual clues to help your child figure out the words like there are when your child is reading. Therefore, stealth dyslexia usually shows up in writing rather than reading.

Last, but not least, stealth dyslexia tends to remain hidden because of a child's high intellectual capabilities. The Eide Neurolearning Blog has an excellent article about stealth dyslexia located at:
http://eideneurolearningblog.blogspot.com/2005/09/stealth-dyslexia-when-writing-is.html.

The Eide Neurolearning Blog says, "The key feature of the stealth dyslexic is an enormous gap between written and oral expression. For individual stealth dyslexics, there are a range of dyslexia-related traits which can contribute to writing difficulties (also known as dysgraphia)."

When your child has stealth dyslexia, his written expression is less sophisticated than his spoken expression. Your child probably uses a broad vocabulary, descriptive words, and expresses himself well while talking. Your child has the ability to express himself well with words, but struggles when trying to write his words on paper.

Your child's writing may be riddled with spelling errors, grammatical errors, and may use simplistic language to communicate ideas because writing is a significant challenge for children with stealth dyslexia.

Therefore, if your child seems highly intelligent, but has very sloppy writing, hates writing, or writes at a level well below his intellectual capabilities, you might want to obtain a comprehensive neuropsychological evaluation from a highly qualified provider to determine if your child has hidden characteristics of dyslexia.

Often a child with stealth dyslexia has outgrown elementary remediation programs before his dyslexia is diagnosed. Therefore, if your child is a mature-for-his-age middle schooler or is in high school, you'll want to choose the more sophisticated remedial programs for reading (like Lexia). You'll definitely want to consider the use of a multi-syllable reading program as discussed later in this book.

Take the time to preview demo software and program materials when selecting programs for your older child. Try to experience the software as your child will perceive it. Think about whether the program is presented with mature, straight-forward instruction, or in a fun, game-like format. Be certain the program you choose is not like a baby-game, and make sure the program won't make your child feel like he's demoted to an elementary education.

If your child is still young (a less mature middle schooler or upper elementary age), go ahead and approach dyslexia remediation as you would for ordinary dyslexia using a robust and comprehensive phoneme awareness program. There are more program choices at the elementary level for teaching phonemic awareness skills, so the sooner you get started, the more options you will have for your child.

Finding a program that fits well with your child's

mindset and personality is an important step. Choosing a program that suits your otherwise gifted learner can make a significant difference in his willingness to use the program. If your child finds a program "babyish" or annoying, he isn't going to want to use it.

By the same token, you should be open and honest with your child about the sneaky, hidden aspect of stealth dyslexia. Make sure your child understands that instruction in the basic phonemes is necessary for figuring out multi-syllable words and for writing.

I highly recommend being straight-forward with your child. Tell him he is intelligent, so it wasn't evident to anyone that he didn't understand the structure of words well enough to write easily.

Explain that not having phonemic awareness and the ability to figure out words he's never seen before can affect him adversely as he gets older, so going back to the basics will make him even smarter about words. Let your child know his advanced vocabulary has allowed him to move ahead in school even without understanding the basics.

I find that kids generally receive the remedial programs fairly well if they understand that sheer intelligence got them as far as they are now and if they understand the difficulties they may face if they never learn the skills needed for decoding big words. If your child understands the purpose behind studying the phonemes and syllabication of words, he is more likely to embrace the remedial programs.

Stealth dyslexia is in fact true dyslexia that was hidden for longer than usual. Being dyslexia by any name, it still requires the same method of instruction. Since the remedial instruction is precisely the same as for simple dyslexia, I won't provide any additional program information here. However, I will add that your child may go through the remedial programming for dyslexia at a faster pace than many kids.

Thus, remediating a child's stealth dyslexia at home is

often an excellent idea because you don't have to slow down your child's academic progress otherwise. If your child has barreled forward so far, there is no sense in halting his momentum now.

It's never a good idea to slow down any child's academic progress, but most schools use a pull-out program for reading remediation, which means students are missing other instruction while in reading class. If you have your child work in one of the computer-based programs discussed later in this book, he may be able to learn the phonemes without any other changes to his schooling.

However, if the stealth dyslexia is impacting your child's performance in school, look for assistive technology or accommodations to help your child stay on track educationally. There is an entire chapter about these types of supports and services in the "Reading and Writing Accommodations" chapter, so check out your options there to help your child stay on track.

If your child has stealth dyslexia and he is in public or private school, you may very well be able to achieve full remediation through weekend, holiday, and summer breaks. By having your child work through a remedial skills program every non-school day and in the evenings before bed, he will be able to move forward with little disruption to his schooling. The more you can do at home, and the more quickly your child can master the skills, the less his stealth dyslexia will affect his overall academic progress.

Double Deficient Dyslexia

Just like "stealth dyslexia," the term "double deficient dyslexia" describes a variation of true dyslexia. As with all forms of neurologically-based dyslexia, double deficit dyslexia has, at its heart, a lack of phonemic awareness.

When initially introduced as a term, double deficient dyslexia referred solely to a condition where the child had a lack of phonemic awareness and a slow neurological processing speed. Processing speed deficits show up in rapid naming tests and other tests of neurological processing speed. When coupled with deficiencies in phonemic awareness, a processing speed deficit can make reading much more difficult because the child can't think fast enough to figure out what he's reading as he is decoding the words.

Truthfully, there are a number of neurological deficits which may co-exist with a lack of phonemic awareness. Thus, I think of "double deficient dyslexia" as a form of dyslexia where a lack of phonemic awareness is coupled with a physical (vision-based) disability or a cognitive deficit. While simple dyslexia by itself is fairly easy to remediate, relatively speaking, the addition of any other disability complicates the remediation process.

For example, if a child has attention deficits and phonemic awareness, he is going to have more difficulty learning to read. If a child has visual processing problems or any other disability, coupled with a lack of phonemic awareness, then teaching the child to read can become difficult. While physical issues such as scotopic sensitivity or visual-perception issues that can be corrected with glasses are a "quick fix," it's often difficult to pinpoint conditions that coexist, causing remediation to be more difficult to achieve.

Truthfully, trying to remediate dyslexia—as an isolated lack of phonemic awareness—often fails because a parent has not considered all areas of physical or cognitive need within her child. Seldom is an isolated lack of phonemic awareness the only disability. Dyslexia accompanied with other cognitive deficiencies is more common than you may think, which contributes to the confusion surrounding remedial programs, products, and services.

Thus, if your child is having significant struggles with learning to read, even when being taught using a proven program for overcoming dyslexia, you should seek a comprehensive neuropsychological evaluation to determine the full scope of your child's learning disabilities and/or learning needs.

A big clue that you should seek a comprehensive evaluation is if you are feeling desperation because your child is not making meaningful progress in reading. If your child has multiple deficits compounding his dyslexia, it will be invaluable to identify each of his specific learning needs.

Unfortunately, when double deficient dyslexia is present, it is more likely that traditional schools will fail to make good progress teaching your child to read. Typical reading remediation protocols will not bring forth skillful reading abilities if your child has an additional area of need that is not being strengthened.

Multi-Dimensional Dyslexia

Just like stealth dyslexia and double deficient dyslexia are forms of true dyslexia, "Multi-dimensional Dyslexia" is a variation of true dyslexia. I use the term Multi-dimensional Dyslexia to refer to reading difficulties that have multiple areas of learning disability, which significantly hinders the reading remediation process. I used to call this "severe dyslexia," but I think the term "Multi-dimensional" describes this form of dyslexia in a more meaningful way.

Multi-dimensional dyslexia is present when a child has phonemic awareness deficits coupled with more than one of the physical and/or perception problems listed previously. This includes phonemic awareness deficiencies coexisting with attention deficits, processing speed problems, memory deficits of any kind, executive function deficits, etc.

Multi-dimensional dyslexia is more difficult to both identify and remediate. Identification requires a comprehensive neuropsychological evaluation by a highly qualified neuropsychologist. The best place to find a fabulous evaluator is among those who know what good and bad evaluations look like.

One of my favorite resources for referrals is the Council of Parent Attorneys and Advocates (COPAA) - http://www.copaa.org/find-a-resource/find-an-attorney/. Special Education attorneys and advocates deal with public school problems, and they routinely seek independent evaluations to help their clients determine the root causes of a child's learning problems.

Since Special Education attorneys have to acquire solid and comprehensive evaluations to force schools to properly address a child's needs, they know who provides the best evaluations in the local area. The attorneys know which evaluators will do a comprehensive job of evaluating and who will produce a detailed report which will clearly explain your child's needs.

If you go to the COPAA website, look for an attorney or advocate in your state or a nearby adjoining state, then call their office and ask if they can give you the names of recommended neuropsychologists. Ask specifically whom they'd recommend for a comprehensive evaluation for learning disabilities.

Alternately, you can check with your state's National Parent Technical Assistance Center (NPTAC, http://www.parentcenternetwork.org/). The parent centers are advocacy organizations in each state. NPTAC helps parents navigate "the system" in order to obtain supports and services for children who have disabilities.

Your Parent Center can make recommendations for evaluators in your area, but they are not necessarily focused on the quality of the listed providers' evaluations and reports. Your state's National Parent Technical Assistance Center is more of a referral source where anyone willing to provide services may be listed and their name will be given out for referrals. The NPTAC is a good place to receive information on licensed practitioners in your area who provide the type of evaluation you are seeking, but you will need to check references from the provider to determine the quality of his evaluations.

A great place to ask questions about evaluators is within the Learning Abled Kids' support group. You can join the group at:
http://groups.yahoo.com/neo/groups/LearningAbledKids/.
In the group, you can search the archives for past posts about evaluators or inquire about a specific doctor you have found through another avenue to see if anyone has used that doctor. You can also ask within the group if anyone has a great evaluator they can recommend in your geographic area or state.

Once you've obtained a comprehensive evaluation and received the written report, you'll want to hunt through your evaluation report to find each and every neurological deficit or learning problem your child has. If your child has deficits in memory, you'll want to use a memory enhancement program. If your child has a slow processing speed, you'll want to use a program that will improve his thinking speed. If your child has phonemic awareness deficits, he'll need detailed instruction as described later in this book.

Whether or not your child has multi-dimensional dyslexia, it's wise to also consider evaluations for visual problems and auditory processing problems if your child demonstrates any symptoms of those conditions. Identifying all of the remedial therapies and instructional elements your child needs will maximize your child's chances for educational success.

My older son has multi-dimensional dyslexia. Identifying and addressing each of my son's needs was no small task. Let me encourage you though—through homeschooling, we were able to purposefully and diligently remediate each area of difficulty he had, which has enabled him to be academically successful throughout high school and college.

My son is a far cry from our public school's prediction that he would "never learn to read well" and their declaration, "He is not college material!" My son has overcome his learning disabilities in a mighty way. This year he will graduate Magna Cum Laude from the university with a B.S degree in his chosen field of science, has been inducted into multiple honors societies, and is on his way to a fulfilling career.

While addressing each of my son's needs was time-consuming and required determination and faith, he was worth every minute of time and effort we poured into him. I would say, if you similarly love your child with all your heart—like I do my son—then you can and should identify and tackle each of your child's specific learning needs.

Facing learning problems head-on is the best way to give your child hope for a great future. Focusing on what your child CAN do will keep his self-esteem positive, and it will give him hope that overcoming his struggles is possible.

Whatever your child's identified needs are, if you work on overcoming them, you can help your learning abled kid experience academic success.

Cognitive Enhancement for Multi-Dimensional Dyslexia

I'm including this section in this "Dyslexia Soup" chapter because cognitive issues add significant barriers when attempting to remediate dyslexia. If your child has been diagnosed with problems in his executive functioning, working memory, processing speed, or his ability to focus his attention, etc., I'd recommend having your child use a cognitive enhancement program to improve learning across all subjects.

While none of the neurological conditions listed here are mistaken for dyslexia, deficits in each of these areas can have a significant effect on your child's overall ability to learn from the instruction he receives. Since cognitive enhancement programs have been shown by research to enhance processing speed, memory, attention to detail, and the underlying executive functions, strengthening your child's cognitive functions can make learning easier for your child.

Processing speed, memory, attention, perception, and the executive functions affect every aspect of your child's learning. Physical issues like scotopic sensitivity or ocular motor deficits affect a child's ability to physically read printed matter, but cognitive skills are the foundation for learning. If your child does not have solid cognitive skills, learning to read can be quite difficult.

That's not to say that you must address underlying cognitive skills, but you should be aware that enhanced cognitive skills equal enhanced learning ability. Therefore, addressing cognitive skills before or in conjunction with remedial instruction is wise.

Improvement is likely if you have your child work regularly with a cognitive enhancement program. If you're homeschooling and have time on your side, I'd recommend beginning a cognitive enhancement program at the same time you begin remedial reading instruction. The two will not conflict with each other, and doing both simultaneously will allow you to shorten the overall time you will spend in remedial reading instruction.

If your child is in a traditional school, then using a cognitive enhancement program as an activity on non-school days, school breaks, or during the summer will offer some degree of improvement. It should be noted though, daily use of a cognitive enhancement program is the proven protocol for providing meaningful improvements.

Each program I mention below has research data backing the effectiveness of the programs. We used Lexia's Cross-Trainer Programs with our boys, but there are many other programs to choose from now than there were when we began working on enhancing our boys' cognitive skills.

For young children, I like Brainware Safari by the creators of Fast ForWord, and the Lexia Cross-Trainer programs. For upper middle school or high school students, I prefer BrainBuilder by Advanced Brain Technologies or Lumosity, written by a team of neuroscientists. Each of these programs has scientific research proving the effectiveness of the programs when used as designed and used regularly.

Lexia's Cross-Trainer programs are the cognitive enhancement programs we used. There are two Cross-Trainer programs: Visual Spatial and Logical Reasoning.

The Visual Spatial (V-S) program works on enhancing visualization, visual memory, spatial orientation and perspective as well as other visual skills. The V-S program can help with your child's understanding of perspective and orientation when it comes to proper orientation of the letters when he's writing. In other words, if your child has reversals in his lettering or visual-perception issues, then the Visual-Spatial program can help.

The Logical Reasoning (LR) program strengthens the executive functions of organization, sequencing, pattern recognition, etc. The LR program is a "must do" if you are going to use the Lexia programs for your child's cognitive enhancement. Organization, planning, sequencing, and other executive functions are required for good reading decoding and word encoding while writing.

If your child has been diagnosed with executive function deficits, you will need to use a cognitive enhancement program of some kind. Lexia's Logical Reasoning program is a good place to begin.

I say the Logical Reasoning program is a good place to begin and it is recommended for any child with dyslexia because it is a relatively short-duration program to complete. There is research behind its effectiveness for the skills it covers. There are new programs on the market for brain training, so although Lexia's Cross Trainer programs are time-tested, I'm not sure they are as comprehensive as some of the newer programs.

It is important to note that you won't see much progress if your child's use of a program is sporadic. Brain training must be undertaken daily and diligently to bring about effective changes in your child's cognitive processes.

Programs should be used for about 30 minutes once or twice per day, particularly if you're homeschooling. If you use the program twice per day, I highly recommend one session in the morning (at the beginning of your school day) and another session just before bed.

If your child is in traditional school and willing, you can have your child practice each evening instead of playing video games, watching TV, or participating in other screen-time activities. Do what you can to work cognitive enhancement into your child's schedule. You may find this is one area of remediation your child feels is fun and not like schoolwork at all.

At the writing of this book, the above mentioned options are some of the best currently available. Since technology is constantly changing, you may want to undertake a search to see if there are new, more robust solutions you can use at home for cognitive enhancement.

Regardless of whether you find newer, better programs, the key is to realize you don't have to feel helpless in meeting your child's needs. If your child is struggling due to disabilities, you can find solutions for working with your child at home.

You Can Help Your Child Overcome True Dyslexia

While all of what we've covered so far may feel intimidating for you, let me say: if you can read, speak, and write then you can teach your child how to read, even if he has neurologically-based, multi-dimensional dyslexia. Providing the type of instruction that is needed to overcome dyslexia is not rocket science. It requires repetitive teaching and consistency in providing instruction, but the content you need to teach your child involves letters and sounds. Trust me... I taught my son. Other parents have taught their learning abled kids, and you can teach your child.

If your child has double deficient dyslexia or multi-dimensional dyslexia, your child needs robust, full-immersion reading remediation. The best way I know to address the full range of needs is to homeschool unless you can afford a private, full-time program at a specialized school. If the thought of homeschooling terrifies you, please know it terrified me too!

Before you dismiss homeschooling as an option though, I would ask you to read the book, "*Overcome Your Fear of Homeschooling*," first. You will learn about the many benefits of homeschooling a learning abled kid, many of which you probably haven't considered before.

There are many merchants, school administrators, and teachers who think teaching a child with dyslexia is too difficult for a parent, but that is a perception, not a proven fact. Teachers and administrators don't want to feel like their training isn't worth much if they fail to teach your child, but you can succeed. One administrator at our school scoffed at me by saying I was "playing school," but I can tell you that the instruction required to overcome dyslexia is not over your head if you can read this book.

Merchants want you to think you must have their programs. Tutors and certified teachers want you to think teaching a child with true dyslexia to read requires highly specialized skills, so that you'll hire them to teach your child. School personnel may feel threatened if they think their jobs are in jeopardy when parents are better able to meet a child's needs than highly trained teachers.

Private schools provide the service at a hefty fee because the instruction takes one-on-one or very small group teaching. Public schools are required by federal law to provide appropriate instruction, but they are seldom effective in actually teaching a child to read well because they aren't equipped to provide every child who has dyslexia with one-on-one instruction.

Whatever the issues, perceptions, or fears are that drive other people to scoff at parents who take matters into their own hands, the problems are theirs—not yours. Given that one-on-one instruction is at the heart of the proven methods for teaching children with dyslexia to read, and it takes many hours of instruction, doing the job yourself is often the most cost-effective and time-efficient means for meeting the needs of your child.

While completely overcoming dyslexia may take a long time, if you can address one or two primary areas of remediation at a time, you CAN help your child. The biggest key is to be consistent and diligent in providing remedial instruction in the various areas of cognitive deficit which impact your child's learning.

If your child must remain in traditional school, then I highly recommend using one of the computer-based reading remediation programs on a daily basis until your child can read fluently. For best results repeat any program once, then use a more advanced program.

Using a comprehensive cognitive enhancement program on a daily basis will improve your child's cognitive functioning across all subject areas. You can learn more about improving your child's cognitive processing speed at: http://learningabledkids.com/learning_disability_ld/memory _processing_speed_brain_based.htm.

In one sense, teaching a child with dyslexia how to read is a difficult task, but that is only because of the amount of repetition and the multisensory nature of the instruction required. People don't really know much about the needed instruction because they've never had a prior need to know.

However, the individual teaching tasks themselves are extremely easy to do. If you can say the sounds of the letters and have access to carpet, sand, a pan with soap, etc., you can teach your child to read. It really is that simple.

The key is to realize your child's education is up to you to provide, whether or not your child is in public school. Yes, the schools are supposed to provide a viable education, but they frequently fail to do an adequate job. You and your child will suffer if your child does not learn the core academic skills. Thus, you must take responsibility for insuring that your child gets the education he needs.

Also be aware of your child's need for improved working memory skills, processing speed, visual-spatial awareness, etc., as a critical factor in helping your child overcome multi-layered learning disabilities. If you remain singularly focused on dyslexia, you will limit your child's future success. Your willingness to tackle all areas of need will enhance your child's chances for making good academic progress.

I think one of the biggest takeaways I'd like you to gain from this book is that you are in charge of your child's educational outcomes, and you can help your child. I started with no skills or background in overcoming learning disabilities, yet we were able to achieve great outcomes for my son.

Just like we did and like many other parents have done, I know you can help your child have a better educational outcome. YOU can do this!

WHY PUBLIC SCHOOLS FAIL

Sometimes parents who homeschool wonder if their learning abled kid would be better off going to a public school, expecting the school will help their child. Parents with children struggling in public school wonder why the public school isn't able to teach their child to read, and some wonder if they should homeschool instead. What's going on here?

Let's examine some issues with traditional schools as a matter of clarification. It might help you decide if a change in your child's school provisioning is the answer to your child's learning woes. If you're homeschooling and you have no plans to enroll your child in a traditional school, you can skip this chapter. It is all about traditional schools, their reading program implementations, and issues therein.

Our first question might be, "Why do so many schools fail to use proven programs or fail to effectively teach children with dyslexia to read when we've known for decades how to teach reading skills to these children?"

Schools fail to teach children to read for various reasons, but one thing is clear: there are significant problems within many public schools. The problems which may or may not exist in your local school will require you to undertake a bit of investigation to determine what outcomes exist for students with learning disabilities in reading.

Let us begin by talking about school personnel's perceptions. From there, we'll discuss classroom observations, regression, and ways you might research your school's performance further. If your school does a decent job with education in general, you may be able to get viable services for your child if you can identify specific problems and solutions for those problems.

Public School Personnel's Perceptions

If I had a dime for every time a parent told me, "Our school says they don't recognize dyslexia," or "Our school says they don't deal with dyslexia," I'd be a millionaire! If your child's teacher, administrator, or special education coordinator has given you a similar excuse, they are ignorant about dyslexia and the Federal Individuals with Disabilities Education Act guidelines.

IDEA Regulations: Part 300 / A / 300.8 / c / 10 specifically says, "Specific learning disability means a disorder in one or more of the basic psychological processes involved in understanding or in using language, spoken or written, that may manifest itself in the imperfect ability to listen, think, speak, read, write, spell, or to do mathematical calculations, including conditions such as perceptual disabilities, brain injury, minimal brain dysfunction, **dyslexia**, and developmental aphasia."

There it is right there! Schools cannot legally ignore dyslexia as a diagnosis when it is specifically listed in the federal regulations as a learning disability that schools must address. The Federal Definitions 20 U.S.C. section 1401(30)(B) also says,

"TITLE 20—EDUCATION § 1401

(30) Specific learning disability.

(A) In general

> *"The term "specific learning disability" means a disorder in 1 or more of the basic psychological processes involved in understanding or in using language, spoken or written, which disorder may manifest itself in the imperfect ability to listen, think, speak, read, write, spell, or do mathematical calculations.*

(B) Disorders included

> *"Such term includes such conditions as perceptual disabilities, brain injury, minimal brain dysfunction, **dyslexia**, and developmental aphasia."*

There it is again! Imagine that! Dyslexia is a federally recognized learning disability, but public schools say they don't recognize it. Pete Wright of Wrightslaw.com says, "'dyslexia' has **always** been listed as a specific learning disability in the law." What is wrong with this picture?

Either school personnel are truly that ignorant about dyslexia, even with all we know about dyslexia these days, or they are counting on parents' ignorance when shirking responsibility for educating the child. I shudder to think it's either one, so I'll let you draw your own conclusions about your school.

If your public school will be educating your child, you need to arm yourself with insights about dyslexia (which you are doing while reading this book). You'll need to become knowledgeable about the federal special education regulations and your child's educational rights, then actively advocate for your child because your child's future is at stake.

If your school has given you some song and dance about how they don't deal with dyslexia, I'd suggest writing a letter citing the above legal language. Tell them in no uncertain terms that you expect them to provide your child with an appropriate and proven reading program in addition to other necessary educational programs and supports. Dyslexia is a recognized learning disability, period.

Classroom Observation

If your child is attending a traditional school where he is struggling to learn, he may or may not be receiving enough reading instruction. If you can arrange it, you might want to schedule a class observation with your child's school during his reading resource time.

When my child was in public school and attended their Reading Resource program, we expected he would learn to read. On the contrary, after five years in public school, our private neuropsychologist evaluated our son and found he still could not read beyond a kindergarten level.

Being concerned about our son's lack of meaningful educational progress, I performed an observation of his reading class. I created a pie chart divided up into five minute segments. Every five minutes I wrote down what was occurring in the classroom in the slice of the pie that corresponded with the time on the clock.

My observations shocked me! Between arrival, getting settled, getting materials ready, and the kids asking the teacher what they were going to work on that day, about 10 minutes of the 50 minute period was consumed before reading instruction began. A 10-minute chunk of time was lost on the departure end of the class period with the kids packing their book bags, lining up to go, and leaving.

When you shave 10 minutes off at the beginning of the period and 10 minutes off at the end of the period, a 50 minute class only allows 30 minutes of meaningful instruction. It gets worse from there.

When reading instruction began, the teacher divided the

six children into two groups that would work with her as threesomes. During the 15 minute segment my son's group was receiving instruction, the teacher asked my son six questions. His one-on-one instructional time equated to approximately six minutes out of that 50 minute period.

The kids in the group working with the teacher were not always paying attention when it was another's turn. The kids who were working independently did a lot of looking around, and it was obvious—since they couldn't read—the silent reading they were supposed to be practicing wasn't really happening.

Our school administrators believed the kids were receiving 50 minutes of instruction per day, but observation showed it was far less than that. Our school was so sure of themselves and so confident they were doing "all that can be done" that they told us our son would likely "never read well," and they told us "you just need to lower your expectations."

After my eye-opening observations, I realized my son was receiving about six minutes of direct instruction five days per week. That's 30 minutes per week. It was NO WONDER he wasn't reading even though he was attending a daily reading program.

Thus, if your child is in public school and receiving reading services, particularly if you are not seeing meaningful progress in your child's reading ability, I would implore you to schedule an observation of your child's reading instruction. An observation will help you determine the extent of your child's direct reading instruction.

An observation will be helpful whether you observe similar limitations in teaching or not. Your child may be receiving more instruction, but isn't fully engaged. Maybe the program isn't a multi-sensory, direct, and explicit reading program. You won't know what your child's reading instruction is like without observing his class.

Our school was using the Herman Method at the time,

which is a proven reading program. After my observation, I contacted Renee Herman, creator of the Herman Method for reading, via telephone. Renee was very direct in telling me that our school was not using her program properly, and it would never work as it was being provided!

A child requires one to two hours of direct instruction (one-on-one) every school day in order to learn to read using the Herman program. Our school had selected a "proven program," but they were not using the program properly.

Which leads me to ask you, if your child is in public school:

- Do you know what kind of reading instruction your child is receiving? Is the school using a proven program?

- If the school is using a proven program, are they using the program properly? Is their implementation consistent with the methods used during the research that proved the effectiveness of the program?

- Is your child's school providing reading instruction with sufficient intensity to bring about meaningful educational progress?

Public school programs are often not intense enough, not provided one-on-one, and not properly implemented. Occasionally, a school will use a specific, sequential reading program, but the program has not been PROVEN to work for children who have clinically diagnosed dyslexia.

With breaks in instruction and other issues, it's no wonder kids with dyslexia continue to fall through the cracks in many public schools. The children fall further-and-further behind their peers in spite of well-documented methods and the availability of proven programs for teaching them.

I have spent quite a bit of time analyzing why school programs don't work, why tutoring doesn't work, and why at-home instruction usually works. I've listened to countless stories from parents across the country who have joined the Learning Abled Kids' Support Group.

Whatever the case may be at your child's school, an observation will help you understand the instruction your child is actually receiving as opposed to what the school says he's receiving. Whether your child's program is the wrong type of program, isn't being used properly, or doesn't provide a sufficient level of direct instruction, insights you gain during an observation will help you determine how to fill in your child's instructional gaps.

With your new awareness, you might be able to make suggestions to your child's school about how they need to modify your child's program to improve his academic progress. If they don't want to make any changes, you may need to arm yourself with some heavy duty advocacy skills to convince your child's school to make changes. We'll talk about advocacy more in a minute.

If needed, you can build upon the school's program by working with your child at home. Whatever route you end up taking, being aware of what is or isn't working will help you make good educational decisions on behalf of your child.

Teaching a child with dyslexia how to read boils down to consistent, daily, one-on-one, step-by-step reading instruction provided using programs proven to work for children with specific learning disabilities in reading or clinically diagnosed dyslexia. When programs are implemented properly, using multisensory teaching methods and provided with sufficient intensity, children with dyslexia can learn to read well.

Researching Your School's Track Record

If your classroom observations find no specific problems to correct, it would seem on the surface that your child's school is doing an adequate job of teaching Learning

Abled Kids to read. Are they doing an adequate job?

Schools are required to test students, track educational progress and report their data to the state and U.S. Departments of Education. Given this is the case, it's possible to determine your school system's overall track record for successfully meeting the needs of children with learning disabilities, and—if your child is in public school— you should be able to study your child's annual testing results to see if your child is making adequate yearly progress.

Let's start our data-based investigation by looking at your school system's track record. The main data you can look at is your school's scores and rankings for typical students, scores and rankings for students with disabilities, and the dropout rates. Students with disabilities drop out at a much higher rate than the general student population, so high dropout rates are often an indication of inadequacy in meeting the educational needs of the students.

Three things to keep in mind when you're looking at your school system's data:

1) The school's data is self-reported and is therefore subject to schools wanting to look better on paper than they really are.

2) There have been numerous scandals regarding schools cheating on tests when administering them, so any sudden improvements in scores should be examined along with other indicators. For example, if a school has suddenly improved the academic performance of its students, there should be a similar and corresponding jump in graduation rates, higher GPAs, and a decrease in the dropout rate.

3) There have been accusations in some districts of errors in the reported data. There may be over inflation of grades, reported test scores may not reflect actual student performance, and dropout data

has been particularly suspect due to school districts' different ways of deciding if a student has dropped out or not. For dropout rates, I prefer to look at the size of the school's incoming freshman class and the size of the graduating class four years later. The bottom line is that any child who began ninth grade and did not finish high school either moved, died, or dropped out of school. One could reason that a relatively similar number of students will move out of a district as move into a district. Therefore, unless there is something that results in a huge population boom or mass exodus, then moving students should not be a major factor. One could also reasonably assume that the number of students who die will be minimal.

These three cautions are not to say your school is manipulating their data, but be aware that you can't simply glance at the published data and assume your child's school is fabulous based solely upon any single piece of data. If your child has been in school for several years, hasn't learned to read and is still struggling mightily, then that is a good indicator that your child's education is inadequate.

The best places to find school-based data are the U.S. Department of Education's website (http://www.ed.gov/), your state's Department of Education website, and your local school district's website. If you're in another country, reference your country's Department of Education entity to see what data you can find about local schools.

When you go to department of education websites, some suggested searches are:

1) Under the "Surveys and Programs" tab on the Ed.gov site, look at the "National Assessment of Educational Progress" data. This is where you'll find statistics specific to each subject (reading, math, etc.) and where you can see the percentage of

students at or above "proficient." For example, in 2013, Georgia reported 34% of its students tested at or above a proficient level in reading. Two-thirds of students in 4th and 8th grade were not proficient in reading.

2) Search for "data table state graduation rate."

3) Search for "data table state dropout rate."

4) Search for "table specific learning disabilities."

When you examine your state's or school's data, see what the data shows for typical students versus students with disabilities. Don't forget to look at the size of the graduating class as compared to the ninth grade class four years earlier to determine the number of students who did not finish high school.

If the data shows your school (district) provides good outcomes for a large portion of the student population, then your question becomes, "What about my individual child?"

To look at your child's individual progress objectively, you need to gather copies of your child's standardized testing for each school year. Also, gather test data from any evaluations performed for eligibility or IEP (Individualized Education Program) meetings.

If your child's school has not provided this data to you in writing along the way, then you will need to send a letter to the school's office requesting they provide you copies of all of your child's standardized and evaluative test results.

Your child's school is required to keep a permanent record for your child, and you are legally entitled to copies of your child's complete educational records. You may have to pay copying fees, but the cost should be minimal as compared to the need to determine if the school is meeting your child's educational needs.

When you have all of your child's test information on hand, analyze the data. When I'm helping a parent analyze her child's progress, we chronologically list each test, the sections on each test, and then list the child's percentile rankings for each subtest. By looking at the data in chronological order, you can see how your child's scores are changing over time.

For example, if your school uses the ITBS (Iowa Test of Basic Skills), your child will have Reading achievement scores for each year. Find your child's NPR (National Percentile Ranking) for each year, and write them down in chronological order—1st grade, 2nd grade, 3rd grade, etc.

Once you've written down the scores, look at your child's achievement trend. Is his NPR trending upward, trending downward, or remaining fairly steady? You want your child's educational ranking to remain steady or trend upward. What you do not want to see is your child losing ground year after year, particularly if it is by a significant margin.

A downward trend is common when a child's educational needs are not being met. Sometimes a child knows the most, as compared to other children his age, the day he enters school and it's all downhill from there!

For example, when my son started public school, his scores ranged from the 67th to the 94th percentile. He was much smarter than his peers when he started school, but after being in school for five years, his scores were down as low as the 18th and 39th percentiles. There was a significant change from where he was when he began school until the time we pulled him out of school. His trend data clearly showed he was getting further behind his peers every year he was in school.

My son wasn't losing learning abilities each year. The school was just totally incapable of educating my son. You don't want this to happen to your child!

Another interesting comparison to make on behalf of your child is to look at any abilities or aptitude testing that has been administered. Aptitude tests determine what your child is capable of achieving. If your child's aptitude testing reveals scores that are far above his achievement scores, then your school is not enabling learning at the level your child is capable of reaching.

Analyzing your child's achievement trends won't tell you why your child's school is not properly educating your child, but the trends do provide insight into whether they are meeting his educational needs. If your child's school is not measuring up, then you should consider ways to help your child outside of school to give your child his best chance in life.

Why Tutoring Fails

Learning regression, or forgetting what has been taught, is one of the biggest drawbacks to receiving lessons one or two days per week from a tutor. The tutoring session itself may be intense, but your child will easily forget his lesson from one week to the next without significant daily reinforcement of the tutorial lessons throughout the week.

Like many parents, and like you may have tried, we hired a tutor for our son. We went to see her weekly and she spent an hour working with my son every Thursday evening. Her teaching was great and my son even liked going, but his reading progress over time was minimal.

As a real eye-opener, I read research by Renee Herman that found children with true dyslexia need one to two hours of direct reading instruction <u>every day</u> for a period of three years—THREE YEARS—on average to be proficient at a sixth grade reading level. I would cite Renee Herman's research for you, but I read her research study more than 15 years ago, and I cannot find it at this time. Renee Herman is the creator of the Herman Method, which has been updated and is available at:

http://www.soprislearning.com/literacy/the-new-herman-method.

Reading Renee's study revealed that, even though our son's tutoring was excellent; we were not likely to see much progress in his reading abilities through tutoring. Tutoring would not provide a sufficient level of instruction unless we went for tutoring every day. We couldn't afford that.

It was at this time my mind began to focus on ideas for providing the necessary, intense, ongoing instruction required to help my son. The need to address his processing speed issues, ocular motor issues, visual-perception issues, and phonemic awareness deficits, coupled with no meaningful progress in public school ultimately led to our homeschooling.

Food for Thought

Viable reading instruction practices have not been put into place in public schools although we've known how to teach kids with dyslexia how to read for more than fifty years. When your child has multiple cognitive deficits in addition to dyslexia, well—I think you can just sail that ship on down the river because the track record shows traditional schools are highly unlikely to adequately meet the educational needs of your child.

Sadly, many schools do not examine their program provisioning, practices, and individual student needs objectively enough to determine why specific students are not benefiting from the programs being used. Many schools just keep doing what they've always done even though data indicates an ongoing failure to educate children with dyslexia.

Therefore, I'd like to make a suggestion to you. Seriously give some consideration to the possibility of homeschooling your child for one to three years. If you are at home and have the availability to homeschool until your child can read, it is an excellent way to go.

If you have doubts about whether you could

homeschool or have questions about the benefits of homeschooling a child with learning challenges, read the book, "*Overcome Your Fear of Homeschooling.*" The book will give you a solid perspective on how homeschooling can help your child overcome his specific learning disabilities. Homeschooling really is a lot easier than you may think.

During the elementary and middle school years, in particular, your child will benefit from an intense, one-on-one instructional program on a daily basis. These are also the best years to homeschool and get your child on track before he begins high school. If you can work with your child intensely to teach him the core academic skills of reading, writing, and math, you can eventually transition him back into a traditional school.

When we began our homeschooling adventure, my goal was simply to make better progress than our public school made. I took a two-week training class in Orton-Gillingham methods and then began working with my sons. Our initial plan was to homeschool only until my older son could read on a sixth grade level (the average literacy level in the U.S.). Since we began when he was in fifth grade, we figured on homeschooling through middle school, then we planned to re-enroll him into public school.

Imagine how astounded I was after our first year of homeschooling when my son had advanced from a kindergarten, letter-recognition level of reading ability, to a sixth grade reading equivalent. We decided to homeschool another year to advance his skills as much as possible.

After our second year of intense reading instruction at home, my son tested at a 10th grade equivalent. We loved homeschooling by this time, so we decided to continue homeschooling through the end of middle school.

After our third year of homeschooling, my son was at a 13+ grade equivalent in seventh grade reading, which is at the same level of understanding as a college student would have when reading seventh grade books. By the time my son reached high school, we loved homeschooling so much none of us had any interest in contending with our public school's short-comings, which were significant.

Continuing to homeschool allowed my son to pull further ahead through dual enrollment courses and CLEP exams. He was able to finish high school and his freshman year of college simultaneously! My son went away to college, is graduating Magna Cum Laude, and it only took him three-years at college to finish his degree.

My son learned to read just fine in spite of the dire predictions of the administrators at our public school who said he'd never read well. All I did was use the Orton-Gillingham methods properly, picked programs to enhance my son's cognitive performance, and made sure he received the therapies he needed.

I taught my son to read well in a couple of years. I was able to accomplish what our public school failed to achieve during the five years they said they were doing "all we can."

It really isn't rocket science. As a mom, I did it, and you can do it too, whether you help your child after school or through homeschooling. The key is to focus on your child's individual needs and to make sure his needs are met.

There are two things which are important for you to focus upon in helping your child overcome his dyslexia:

1. **First, your child's learning progress will improve if you address all areas of need for your child, including areas of cognitive or physical impairment such as slow processing speed, working memory deficits, executive functioning, visual-perception, ocular motor deficits, etc.**

2. **Second, you must implement programs properly and use them diligently on a daily basis in order to enable your child to make good academic progress. If a program is not used properly or daily, your child's progress will suffer.**

If you homeschool your child, you will have the flexibility to provide instruction as intensely as your child can handle. Your child can make faster progress because you can provide a focused instructional program, and you will be keenly aware of your child's academic engagement at any given moment. If he wasn't paying attention, you can easily repeat his instructions without worrying about whether "time is up" and it's time to change classes.

If you decide to keep your child in school, you can provide instruction in the evenings to the degree your child can tolerate additional remedial work in the evenings. You will want to provide instruction to your child on weekends, during holidays, during the summer, and on days when your child isn't already tired from a long day at school in order to help your child make adequate progress.

No matter how you decide to provide the needed reading instruction, your child requires a LOT of direct instruction. You can make the task easier by using a prewritten program package or a computer-based program. We'll talk about specific program options in the upcoming chapters.

Regression

On the problematic end of remediating learning disabilities is learning regression and learning retention as mentioned briefly in the section about tutoring. A lot of forgetting takes place between lessons, particularly when you're using a tutor or your child is in traditional school and has an extended break from schooling (a week or more). Using the practice programs covered in the upcoming "Practice, Practice, Practice" chapter will help minimize your child's learning loss during breaks in instruction.

Ensuring that your child receives intense daily reading instruction, by whatever means, will help your child make more meaningful progress. His learning skills will advance in direct proportion to the amount of time spent working on reading skills or other cognitive enhancement activities.

The estimated 1080 instructional hours (2 hours per day for 180 days per year for 3 years) are required for reading mastery. The number of hours actually needed will vary depending upon the degree of your child's learning regression between lessons, the intensity of your child's daily instruction, as well as the scope of any accompanying areas of learning difficulty which also need remediation.

Advocacy Skills for Public School Provisioning

My guess is that if you're reading this book and your child is in public school, your child's school is not providing an adequate reading program. Your child may seem like he'll never catch up at the rate he's going with your school.

Making sure your child is taught using a proven program, which is properly implemented, is difficult if your child is in a traditional school. If he's not being taught properly, you may need to turn into a Special Education Advocate on behalf of your child.

I highly recommend visiting the "From Emotions to Advocacy" website at: http://fetaweb.org/ and becoming familiar with special education law through Wrightslaw.com and the U.S. Department of Education "Individuals with Disabilities Education Act" (IDEA) website at http://idea.ed.gov/explore/home.

Critical issues and timeframes for you to be aware of under IDEA:

1) Put all of your requests to the school in writing. If you do not make a request in writing, it "never happened." You must have written proof of your requests.

2) Be calm and factual in your communications with your child's school. If you're having difficulty and the school is not following the law, cite the law and let them know you

expect compliance on their part. School personnel suffer no meaningful consequences if they fail to provide your child with a free and appropriate public education (FAPE), so there have been many cases where the school personnel push the limits of the law with disregard to the consequences for your child. This is most likely and most frequent when it comes to testing for disabilities within the legally required time frames (schools tend to drag their feet), and in providing truly individualized programs. It's not uncommon for a school to use the same program for virtually every child with a reading disability with no consideration of each child's need for programs to improve processing speed, memory, etc.

3) Once you have given consent for an evaluation, the school must complete their evaluation within 60 days under the 2004 IDEA guidelines. (See:

http://idea.ed.gov/explore/view/p/,root,regs,300,D,300%252 E301,c,.)

4) After an evaluation has been completed, an IEP providing the needed services for your child is to be put into place within 30 days. (See:

http://idea.ed.gov/explore/view/p/,root,regs,300,D,300%252 E323,c,.)

5) Your child's educational program should be sufficient to provide "adequate yearly progress," which would be at or near one year of academic progress per year of instruction.

For example, if your child's reading skill is at a 2nd grade equivalent (GE) this year, it should be at a 3rd grade equivalent or higher at the same time next year. If it is anything less, your child is falling further behind his peers.

If instruction is intense enough, a child can actually make more than one year of academic progress in one school year, presumably to catch up to peers. Did you know IDEA specifies your child must make adequate progress in the

"general curriculum"? (See:
http://idea.ed.gov/explore/view/p/,root,regs,300,D,300%252
E320,a,.)

These are only basic tips for advocating on behalf of your child. Please visit WrightsLaw, FETAweb, and the IDEA website to become more knowledgeable about your child's educational rights as well as your rights as a parent.

If your child is not making adequate yearly progress, you will need to become a strong advocate for your child. No one has as much vested interest as you do when it comes to making sure your child receives an adequate education.

Your child's teacher and principal may express care and concern, but the bottom line is that your child will grow up, move out of their school, and there is no consequence to them if your child does not learn or graduate from high school. You are the only consistent caretaker and provider for your child across each of his schools and into adulthood.

Therefore, you must be the one who speaks up and advocates for your child's educational needs. If you can't get the school to meet your child's needs, you must take matters into your own hands to make sure your child receives an adequate education. Whether you have to file a due process lawsuit against your school, pay for private services, or teach your child at home, your child is depending on you.

MULTISENSORY INSTRUCTION

The purpose of this chapter is to explain the proven methodology known to work in teaching children with true dyslexia how to read. Multi-sensory instruction and the Orton-Gillingham methodology have been in existence for decades and are proven methodologies for consistently enabling kids with true dyslexia to read.

Remember, true dyslexia includes stealth dyslexia, double deficient dyslexia, and multi-dimensional forms of dyslexia, all of which include a deficit in phonemic awareness.

We'll talk about the details of teaching your child reading with the Orton-Gillingham method in the next chapter, but for now let us begin by talking about multi-sensory instruction. It's important for you to understand what multisensory instruction is so that you can effectively teach your child.

What is Multi-sensory Instruction?

Multi-sensory instruction involves teaching your child while providing auditory, visual, kinesthetic-tactile (large body or hands-on) input all at the same time. In other words, your child will be hearing or saying the concept (auditory) while he sees the related elements (visual) while engaging in an activity that involves large or small body movements (kinesthetic/tactile) while he is learning the concept.

For example, if your child was learning the sound-symbol relationship for the letter "b" through multisensory instruction, he could say the sound /b/ while writing the letter on a large, traditional chalkboard. Your child would be hearing the sound /b/, seeing the letter "b" as he writes it, and he would be engaging muscle-memory by actively writing the letter as he says the sound it represents.

The key to multi-sensory learning is for all of your child's learning pathways to be engaged simultaneously. Your child needs to hear, see, and feel each concept for it to become implanted in his long-term memory.

(As a side note, throughout the book, I will use speech-language notation by placing slashes on each side of a letter or letter combination when the notation represents "the sound of" that letter/combination. So, if I write /s/, you will know it represents the sound of the letter "s," which is ssss.)

Why is Multi-sensory Instruction Important?

Multi-sensory instruction is the primary method of teaching used by the Orton-Gillingham methodology, but more importantly it is critical for a child who has dyslexia. A child who has true dyslexia does not have the same wiring in his brain for processing phonemes (sounds as they relate to letter symbols) as typical readers.

Functional MRIs have been used to examine the brain activity of readers who do and don't have dyslexia. It has been revealed that children with true dyslexia process written text in their frontal lobe whereas typical readers process text in the language center of their brain.

Since a child with true dyslexia has a different way of processing written information in his brain, he will not learn to read using traditional, print-based teaching methods. Your child must see, hear, and feel the sounds as they relate to the letters in order to process and learn the sounds and their related symbols.

Teaching a child using multi-sensory activities can be a lot of fun! It is hands-on learning, which you can easily provide at home through fun and engaging activities like finger painting, writing in a pan of soap bubbles or sand, writing huge letters on a chalkboard, etc.

Conversely, it is more difficult for a traditional school to provide this type of instruction in a classroom full of children. The hands-on activities and speaking out loud nature of multisensory instruction tends to be disruptive if the class has a number of students or is "too active."

Thus, in a traditional school your child is more likely to be instructed in a sit down, don't move, and be quiet manner. Needless to say, your child will have more difficulty learning in a traditional, "sit at your desk and don't talk" school environment.

If, however, you can teach your child to read using multisensory instruction at home, he will be able to function better in a traditional classroom. My son, who has severe dyslexia, is able to function fabulously in his traditional college classes now that his reading disability has been overcome.

The most difficult aspect of multi-sensory instruction is coming up with activities that are simultaneously auditory, visual, and kinesthetic. I'll share some of the activities we used to give you some ideas, but you may also want to check out the three web page series of activities on the Learning Abled Kids' website beginning with

http://learningabledkids.com/multi_sensory_training/page22-auditory2.htm.

The biggest key to remember is that your child must be moving, seeing, and hearing the content simultaneously.

Generally speaking the moving and hearing parts are pretty easy. Your child says the represented sound out loud as he writes the corresponding letters. Choosing the method or media used to write the letters while saying them is where your challenge of providing variety comes into play.

Our mainstay for multisensory instruction was a traditional chalkboard, which we hung at chest-level for my boys (when they were younger). We used colored chalks for writing the letters in a HUGE format on the board.

When my boys were young, we bought buckets of the thick sidewalk chalk because the thick sticks allowed our boys to be vigorous with their writing. They could say the letter sounds loudly while writing without worrying about breaking the chalk.

We also have a standard whiteboard we used in a similar fashion. The whiteboards are smooth, so the feel of writing on the board is not quite as multi-sensory in nature as writing on a traditional chalkboard. The whiteboard did allow for freer, smoother writing. It was beneficial as we moved toward writing somewhat smaller letters for the purpose of handwriting. On our whiteboard, we wrote letters that were six to twelve inches high.

We performed what we called "carpet writing" where my boys used their bare feet to write the letter shapes in our carpet with their big toes. Writing with bare feet in a sandbox is a great variation too. We also performed fingertip writing on velvet pillows, or large squares of felt.

Liquid soap in a pan is always a fun activity, and I think it was probably my boys' favorite multi-sensory movement. To use the soap-in-a-pan method, get an ordinary sheet pan, squirt some liquid soap into the pan, and smear the soap around rapidly until it forms a white film with very tiny bubbles. Don't add water, or the soap may become too thin to write letters within.

Sheet pans can be filled with rice, sand, or shaving cream to write in, but for either rice or sand, I prefer a deeper pan like a roasting pan. You have less spillage and clean-up after your lesson if you use a deeper pan. Placing a washable tablecloth under the pan is always a good idea. Alternately, you can go outside and write in the sand in a sandbox or write in the dirt.

One of my son's favorite activities was painting, whether we used finger paints or a paint and a brush. You can also use crayons on construction paper. The construction paper has a rougher texture than traditional writing paper, so it becomes more multi-sensory than traditional paper and pen.

There are also some great apps you can use with a computer tablet these days which allow your child to trace letters on the screen with his finger. You have to be careful to get apps or programs that practice letter sounds—not the names of the letters. You do not want your child practicing the name of the letter, because he will need to know the sound the letter represents when he's reading.

For example, with the sound /b/, your child would learn the quick "buh" sound you associate with the letter when you're reading, but the sound you speak would be /b/ without the "uh" sound. Consider the words bug, boot, bird, best, buns, etc. The sound of "b" is a very short "buh," and not "bee." The only time the letter "b" is coupled with the "bee" sound is when it is followed by the letter "e," as in be, bee, begin, etc., but not always!

Best, bed, and bend are three examples of "b" words where the "be" combination does not represent the "bee" sound. And, yes, instruction needs to be very precise for your child to be able to decode increasingly sophisticated words. This is why it's beneficial to use a scripted program to be certain you've covered all of the possible sound-symbol phonemes. We'll talk more about instructional specifics and programs in the upcoming chapters.

Last, but not least, you can always use traditional pens and paper to write and say the sounds simultaneously.

However, some children who have fine motor skill deficits will learn their phonemes faster and easier while using large body movements over handwriting.

Using traditional paper and pens (or pencils) isn't nearly as fun or "cool" as using other materials, but it is practical for helping your child learn to write on paper. In the upcoming chapter about writing, we'll cover information about handwriting, but for now just think of handwriting as one option out of many for teaching your child his phonemes.

When beginning your instruction at home, start with the large body-movement activities, and then move toward smaller movements or finer motor skills as your child moves from mastery of the phonemes to mastery of words.

In other words, start by using large body movements to write on chalkboards, whiteboards, carpet, etc. As your child masters each phoneme, you can begin practicing it with hand gestures using finger writing on a rough or textured surface, in sand, rice, shaving cream, etc. Lastly, move to fine motor skills, including actual handwriting.

The progression from large body movement to fine motor skills helps your child gain mastery of the overall shape of the letter before trying to write a well-formed, small letter on paper. The level of physical dexterity for large body movements does not require the preciseness that handwriting requires, so movement from large to small lettering makes success more accessible for your child.

There are other variations of using multi-sensory instruction which involve holding up a card with a phoneme written on it so the child can see it, and the child moves and recites the sound represented. This is a flash-card type of drill where the child is bouncing on a large ball, jumping on a trampoline, rocking in a chair, jumping up and down, clapping or engaging in some movement that is not directly related to the formation of the letters.

These activities are multi-sensory by definition, but I

preferred not to use them very often because they did not invoke the muscle-memory of how to form the letter within the movement. Let's face it—bouncing on a ball or clapping while saying a phoneme does not help the child learn how to write the phoneme. Large-body writing, finger writing, or handwriting does help your child develop the memory of how to write the phoneme.

We did, from time-to-time, engage in the bouncing, jumping, or rocking kinds of drills when working with flashcards, but they were not the mainstay of our program. Using alternate movements can be beneficial to use when your child is particularly tired and you think your child would like a simpler day of lessons or when you are using flashcards for mastery review.

Now that you understand the basics of multi-sensory instruction, let's move into the core requirements for teaching your child how to read. The next chapter introduces the Orton-Gillingham methodology to you as the means for overcoming your child's dyslexia.

ORTON-GILLINGHAM
METHODOLOGY

Would you believe the Orton-Gillingham (O-G) method for teaching children with dyslexia to read has been around since the 1930's? You'd think teaching children with dyslexia to read would be a simple matter of identification and remediation given the proven track record of the Orton-Gillingham method and its longevity.

However, from the ongoing lack of appropriate intervention in schools, it's clear educators and parents alike are confused about dyslexia. Many parents and educators think "We don't know how to overcome dyslexia," when—in fact—we know precisely how to overcome dyslexia and many other conditions that cause difficulty with reading if we sort things out carefully and properly use the right solutions.

When we add public school failures in providing properly implemented Orton-Gillingham programs to the market place confusion about dyslexia and the wide variety of overlapping conditions that need intervention, we end up with the vast majority of children with true dyslexia never receiving the help they need. The school personnel begin to think dyslexia is some mysterious learning disability that can't be remediated very well.

After your child has been evaluated to identify all physical, neurological, perceptual, and cognitive conditions impacting his reading abilities, then a proper solution should be applied for each area of disability. When your child has a lack of phonemic awareness, the Orton-Gillingham methodology is needed to help your child learn this specific skill. Your child may need other therapies or solutions too. Good results come from addressing all of your child's needs one-by-one. See the prior chapters for suggestions related to other types of reading impairments.

The Orton-Gillingham method was developed by Samuel Orton and Anna Gillingham when they worked with seemingly bright kids who struggled immensely in learning to read. The Orton-Gillingham method has been proven to be effective in helping students develop phonemic awareness skills by countless research studies. The O-G method is currently the primary method for overcoming true dyslexia.

Specifically, the O-G method uses multi-sensory instruction to provide direct, one-on-one instruction for each phoneme, syllable, sight word, etc. The method uses explicit and comprehensive instruction to teach every single detail of how to decipher and decode words without leaving any aspect of decoding untaught.

The O-G method is mastery-based, which means you re-teach every phoneme until your child can instantly recall the sound and its representing letters without requiring thinking time, and he can recall the phoneme whenever needed. Your child will demonstrate mastery of any element in the program with automatic recall.

In way of a short example, if you are teaching the phonemes in the word "cat," you teach your child the hard sound /c/, the short-vowel sound /ă/ and the sound /t/. When your child masters each of those phonemes, he will be able to sound out /c/, /ă/, and /t/ quickly and easily, without the need to think deeply to recall the sounds associated with each of the letters. The O-G method also teaches blending skills so your child will learn to blend the /c/, /ă/, and /t/ in order to form the word "cat."

In another quick example, a child would learn that /c/, /ă/, and /p/ form the word "cap." However, when the letter "e" is added, the short /ă/ is changed to the sound of a long /ā/ and the word becomes "cape."

Orton-Gillingham programs also explicitly teach that vowel-consonant-consonant-e words allow the vowel to retain its short-vowel sound. Using our prior example, if two consonants appear together, such as in the word "capped," then the sound of "a" is the short vowel sound /ă/.

While this may seem like simple phonics, mass market phonics programs often lack the required depth of instructional detail and don't use multisensory teaching methods. The O-G method is detailed and specific in teaching which letters change the sounds of other letters, the rules of frequent use, and each and every detail in the rules.

The O-G method is very explicit in teaching vowel-consonant-e (v-c-e) pattern changes, the short-vowel sounds, long vowel sounds, vowel digraphs, etc. Students learn how to sound out words, how to apply rules, and when to apply rules. Additionally, O-G teaches everything through multisensory instruction.

Teaching your child to read using the O-G methodology is by no means rocket science, but it entails a lot of detailed, repetitive instruction. I taught my son. Other parents have taught their kids. You can teach your child.

If you can say short, simple sounds over and over, and you can get your child to repeat them as he writes the letters representing the sound, then you can teach your child using an Orton-Gillingham program. In teaching your child using an O-G program, you can take one of two approaches:

1) You can learn about the O-G methodology, create your own teaching materials, and systematically teach your child phoneme-by-phoneme, syllable-by-syllable, without spending much money at all,

– or –

2) You can purchase a pre-packaged, scripted Orton-Gillingham reading program. You can teach your child directly from the program by following the teaching scripts. Scripted programs usually include teaching materials, which makes your job even simpler.

The primary trade-offs between using a do-it-yourself Orton-Gillingham approach and purchasing a program are as follows:

1) With a do-it-yourself O-G program, you can buy materials (like letter tiles, papers, chalks, etc.) from the least expensive seller you can find. You can use the Orton-Gillingham manual to learn how to implement the method, making your individualized O-G based program relatively inexpensive. Your biggest drawback in creating your own program is that you are more likely to miss or skip some critical sounds, rules, or concepts for application, which may hamper your child's progress.

2) With a scripted, pre-packaged program it is easier for you to just follow directions and do what the program script says. The biggest drawback of using a scripted program is that you are less likely to be able to tailor the program to your child's specific needs, and you may find yourself questioning when to move on versus whether to repeat a lesson again. A secondary drawback of using a scripted program is that virtually all of them are offered in "levels," and the cost of purchasing the program can be significant. Although the cost of a pre-scripted

program is high, it is still cheaper than paying for a tutor. Having the program yourself will enable you to repeat instructions and work with your child for as long as it takes without the hourly charges you'd have with a tutor.

I chose a do-it-myself approach, but I completed a 56-hour Orton-Gillingham training program beforehand. The cost of my training was as much (if not more than) buying a pre-packaged program, but it gave me the ability to use the O-G methods across all subjects. Understanding how to work with your child across all subjects enhances your child's learning (making your child's learning progress faster). The training also helped me understand the importance of each aspect of the O-G methodology.

If you want to be able to help your child in the most effective way possible and can afford it, I'd highly recommend completing an Orton-Gillingham training course, whether you use a scripted program or create your own program. Given that the Orton-Gillingham method is the foundation for most dyslexia remediation programs, understanding the core foundation and reasons behind the methodology can give you greater skill and confidence in teaching your child.

You may be able to find an Orton-Gillingham course locally by contacting your state chapter of the International Dyslexia Association. If you don't have a local training provider, you can obtain training through the Dyslexia Training Institute, the Institute for Multi-sensory Education, or through the Orton Academy's list of qualified training providers.

In lieu of training, you can learn about the Orton-Gillingham Method without completing a training course, by reading *The Gillingham Manual: Remedial Training for Students With Specific Disability in Reading, Spelling, and Penmanship*. This book is the definitive guide to the Orton-Gillingham Method. It is a valuable resource for anyone who wants to understand the methods used to teach children with dyslexia how to read, but it is not light reading.

I'll discuss pre-packaged programs more in the next chapter, so if you know you'd prefer having a done-for-you solution, you may want to jump ahead to the next chapter. The remainder of this chapter contains information about how to teach your child without a scripted program, if you are interested in taking the do-it-yourself route.

Orton-Gillingham instruction is repetitive, and it takes a long time to teach your child every single phoneme in the English language. According to my *Second College Edition American Heritage Dictionary*, there are 232 sound-symbol correlations. The American Heritage Dictionary has one of the most comprehensive tables I've found, so you can't go wrong if you use their table as a checklist for teaching your child. Whatever dictionary you have on hand may have a similar table.

Traditional Orton-Gillingham programs count fewer phonemes because they don't consider every single possibility separately. For example, —ed can either represent the sound of "d" (nailed) or the sound of "t" (stopped). Some programs may count —ed as one phoneme to be taught, and others may count it as two because of the different sounds that —ed can represent.

To provide you with some basic resources, I have created a phoneme checklist table with the most common sound-symbol correlations. The table has checkboxes you can use to check off each phoneme as your child masters it.

I also made some Phonogram Tiles that you can print on cardstock, laminate with adhesive laminate, cut out and use for letter and spelling practice with your child. They are the printable tiles I created for use with my boys when I was teaching them to read.

Lastly, I have also created a set of do-it-yourself sight word flashcards you can print on micro-perfed business cards to make your own flashcards to use with your child.

You will find these three resources at:

http://learningabledkids.com/downloadablepdfs/free-learning-resources-page.htm.

You can find the micro-perfed cards on Amazon by searching for "perforated printer cards." All you have to do is download the PDF file I've provided, buy the perforated cards, print the printable PDF document contents on the cards, then separate the cards for use.

If you don't wish to use "print it yourself" cards, I'd highly recommend purchasing the "Interactive Reading Kit" and the "Student Packet" for **each** reading level on All About Reading's website. If you purchase the interactive kit and each of the student packets, you'll have a complete set of cards with phonemes and sight words to use in teaching your child.

Teaching your child to read using an Orton-Gillingham approach requires explicit teaching of each piece of our language structure, including:

- the letter-sound combinations for every phoneme,

- spelling and sound rules,

- rules for segmenting syllables,

- standard syllables like –sion, re-, and –ing,

- blending and segmenting words, and

- sight word memorization.

Therefore, you will also need a resource for teaching your child spelling rules, syllable rules, etc., unless you know these rules well. Do you know the rules for word division, open syllables, closed syllables, etc.? For example, when segmenting the word "reading," your child will need to know the syllables are "read" and "ing."

If you don't know the rules already, I'd highly recommend getting the Scholastic Book titled, *Teaching*

Phonics & Word Study in the Intermediate Grades," *"Uncovering the Logic of English,* or a similar book that contains all of the rules governing the English Language. Using a book like one of these as a reference will ensure you don't skip essential rules that will help your child read and write words.

As I said before, it isn't rocket science, but it is tedious and time-consuming. It can take 200, 300, or even 500 repetitions of teaching the same letter–sound relationship before a child with true dyslexia can recall the phonemes with automatic mastery. Each element is taught directly, using multi-sensory teaching methods.

If you multiply the number of phonemes to be taught by the number of required repetitions, it is easy to see why your persistence and patience will be tested. It takes a lot of dedication to teach your child to read well if he has the specific learning disability called dyslexia.

However, before you get wigged out and run screaming from the room, I should tell you that you don't have to personally teach every sound-symbol repetition 300+ times. There are tools you can use to enhance your child's progress without personally repeating yourself 200-500 times. You'll still have a lot of repetition in your direct teaching, but let me say now: "THANK YOU, Lord, for computer-based practice programs!"

Thankfully, there are computer programs which are infinitely patient in drilling phonemes repeatedly. Well-designed programs will track your child's mastery and give you a measure of relief from the repetitive nature of the instruction you have to provide.

One-on-one instruction must be provided by you when your child is first introduced to each phoneme and during regular practice intervals to ensure your child is pronouncing and understanding the phonemes correctly. However, computer programs and apps for tablets are great tools for giving your child a significant portion of the needed practice.

You can't rely solely upon the computer programs because voice recognition technology can't always recognize the fine nuances if your child mispronounces a sound. When your child verbalizes closely related sounds like /f/ and /v/, or the sounds /d/ and /t/, it is unlikely a computer will be able to distinguish the slight differences.

If you leave teaching and learning totally up to your child and a computer program, your child may practice a sound incorrectly. It will be even harder for your child to unlearn the wrong way and relearn the sound the right way. Therefore, it's best to introduce each phoneme through one-on-one teaching and to monitor your child's computer-based practice.

It is a blessing to you if you can afford today's technology to cover some of the repetitive instruction, but all instruction can be provided by you using simple materials in your home. We used a couple of computer programs for daily practice, but the programs are a nicety, not a necessity.

If you are prone to beating your head against the wall or screaming like a banshee, I suggest you write a reflective note to yourself before you begin the task of remediating your child's dyslexia. You may think this is an odd suggestion, but trust me... there WILL be days when you will want to bash your head on the wall because you have already taught a particular phoneme fifty-bazillion times!!

Okay, it wasn't fifty-bazillion times or your child would have mastered it by now, but the task of providing repetitive instruction can be tedious and frustrating for those of us who are not blessed with infinite patience. Therefore, you must encourage yourself, and you must resolve to teach your child with love and compassion so he doesn't lose hope.

I recommend you begin by writing yourself a note to express your commitment to this process and your child.

You can write something similar to this:

"Dear Self,

"I love <u>your child's name</u> more than words can say, and I want <u>your child's name</u> to be educationally successful and able to pursue any dreams or goals he has in life. Therefore, I am voluntarily undertaking this task to give <u>your child's name</u> the best future possible.

I promise <u>your child's name</u> I will undertake this task with patience, compassion, and selfless love. I hereby set my mind on working calmly to teach <u>your child's name</u> to read, no matter how many repetitions it takes, and to work with love and patience for as long as it takes for him to learn to read. I will provide compassionate, encouraging, and reassuring instruction.

I love <u>your child's name</u> more than anything, and I will do all I can to instruct him with calm, loving respect."

Signed _____

Put the note in your bathroom or bedroom. When you feel like you are losing your sanity or feel like screaming due to the tedious repetition, go to your room, read your letter aloud, and remind yourself of why you are undertaking this task on behalf of your child. There will be days when it seems like your child will "never" learn, but there will also be days of surprising and rewarding progress.

I know from first-hand experience, at times, working to overcome dyslexia can seem like it will go on forever, but then you'll stop one day and be amazed at the progress your child has made. Progress tends to come in such small increments you don't really notice until you've accumulated sound-symbol mastery for a cluster of phonemes. When you realize your child has fluency with some of the phonemes, it will bring excitement, joy, and a sense of accomplishment for you and your child.

Consider yourself forewarned. Your child will seem to know sound-letter combinations one day, and the next day it will be as if he's never seen the letters before in his life. They say the only thing consistent about the performance of a child with learning disabilities is the inconsistency in performance. While you may find it difficult to believe your child doesn't know a phoneme when he seemed to do so well yesterday, if your child says he doesn't know a sound, he truly can NOT remember.

Once, I had a frustrated parent tell me, "He acts like he doesn't know it, but he did yesterday." Children simply do not "act" like they don't know—they truly don't know. Every child wants to be able to learn, and no child purposefully doesn't remember the phonemes, especially if he thinks he will face the wrath of mom if he can't remember. If your child says he can't remember, that means he simply hasn't mastered the phoneme yet.

Therefore, if you have difficulty with your temper, get ready to buckle down on yourself and wage a difficult internal battle to maintain your personal composure. Getting mad at your child will cause his mind to shut down, and your child will then be unable to remember the day's lessons. You must resolve to maintain a calm, encouraging demeanor throughout your instruction.

After frustrating lessons, you can go cry in your room, but please don't display aggravation and frustration to your child as you repeat, repeat, repeat your teaching. Becoming angry with your child will only damage your relationship or impact your child's self-esteem. Truly, your child feels as frustrated as you do, so as the adult in the room—you are the one who must maintain composure (spoken from experience).

The funny thing about wrestling with the demons of frustration and a lack of patience within yourself is that you will emerge with a level of patience you may never have thought you had. If you do have issues with patience, consider this a great opportunity to exercise your patient demeanor day after day, smiling on the outside and sighing on the inside. Both you and your child can grow immensely by overcoming dyslexia together at home.

If I've given you any doubts about undertaking this task of teaching your child to read, let me tell you—the time you spend teaching your child will be worth every minute of frustration you may feel. You will literally be giving your child a wide-open future, where he can achieve whatever he sets his mind upon. You and your child will gain an immense sense of pride in overcoming dyslexia together.

So, after sharing the realities with you, you're still reading this book? I thought you might throw the book down and run from the room screaming. Since you're still here, I must conclude you still feel committed toward helping your child learn to read in spite of his dyslexia. GOOD FOR YOU!

I think you've made a great decision because I can tell you with 100% certainty that there are many parents who aren't willing to make the personal sacrifice of time or effort to ensure their child learns to read. Unfortunately, the schools have so many kids, they are unable to provide one-on-one instruction to every child that needs it. Therefore, if a child's parents aren't willing to provide the one-on-one instruction, that child is unlikely to learn to read proficiently.

Since we have confirmed that you are willing to teach your child, let us move forward. Throughout this book I will share with you the research I did, the programs we used, and tips for practical implementation of your child's program. If you're going to create your own teaching materials, you can use the printable PDF cards shared earlier in this section, the PDF Checklist, and either a Sitton or Dolch word list for the most commonly used words to teach your child.

The process you will use in teaching your child involves selecting the phonemes you will work on each week, and teaching your child each element until he masters it to the point of automatically responding without hesitation. Begin by teaching letters and their associated sounds. When the letter-sound combinations are mastered, then move to teaching syllables and single syllable sight words. From there move into teaching decoding and blending of multi-syllable words, common words, etc.

I recommend starting with the five short vowel sounds (/ă/ as in bat, /ĕ/ as in bet, /ĭ/ as in bit, /ŏ/ as in bot, /ŭ/ as in but) and teaching each of those until your child has mastered them. You want to begin with the short vowels because vowels appear in *every* word, and the short vowels appear most often. Be sure to teach the short vowel sounds and not the letter names.

As your child masters the sounds with repeated automatic recall, add in new phonemes (new letters and the sounds they represent). Split your lesson time into three parts:

1) Introduction of new sound-symbol phonemes,

2) Concentrated practice of phonemes your child is currently practicing, and

3) Review of all prior sounds your child has mastered.

Only add in one new sound-symbol relationship for each sound-symbol you are moving to the mastery practice.

For example, if you start with, /ă/, /ĕ/, /ĭ/, /ŏ/, and /ŭ/, and your child masters /ŭ/, then you might add in the sound of "b," which is noted as /b/. If your child then masters the /ĕ/, you might add in /d/.

If this were the case, your practice sections for the above case would involve three segments as follows:

1) Introduction of the /d/ with specific practice,

2) Concentrated practice of /ă/,/ĭ/, /ŏ/, /b/ and /d/,

3) Review practice of /ĕ/ and /ŭ/.

For each phoneme you introduce, you will have your child write or create the letter multiple times while simultaneously saying the ***sound*** the letter represents. You can have your child write the letter in a soapy pan, in the carpet with his bare big toe, on a textured fabric with his finger tip, on paper with crayons, or on a standard chalkboard with large arm movements, etc. Practice the newly introduced sound(s) multiple times to help them stick in your child's mind. Remember every repetition of instruction now is one step closer to mastery!

You'll notice for the concentrated practice phase, you will continue to practice the newly introduced sounds too. The additional focus on the new sound-symbols will help your child with memory-recall.

Also, while you may have more or fewer sounds in your concentrated practice section, I would not recommend practicing more than eight sounds in the middle segment of your lesson. The practice period becomes too long, and there is a tendency to practice "lightly" to speed things up. Therefore, keeping the number of sounds you are teaching few in number will allow your child to have an adequate amount of practice with each sound.

During each lesson, practice each sound for 20-25 repetitions, or about 3-5 minutes. If you're practicing with six sounds, that will be an 18-30 minute lesson. That is usually a tolerable amount of time for each teaching segment. Additionally, research by Hermann Ebbinghaus shows you'll hit a "forgetting curve" if instruction isn't broken into short segments with recovery/retention time between teaching segments.

When you get to the third portion of your lesson—the Mastery Review—then you can move very quickly. For this, you will use flash cards. Show your child the symbol, and have your child say the ***sound*** represented by the symbol, not the symbol's name. If your child responds quickly without hesitation, put the card into a "Know It" pile. If your child hesitates, put the card at the back of your card stack so it will come up again in the review. Continue this process until all cards are in the "Know It" pile and there are none left in your hand.

Note: If your child cannot recall a sound for any given symbol, even with ample thinking time, consider switching it back to the instructional segment for sound-symbol phonemes being learned. If your child can't recall it at all, it still needs instructional practice rather than mastery review.

When you're beginning the remedial instruction process, during the Mastery Review phase, you will only have one or two cards in your Mastery Review deck. Your child will be able to go through them very quickly, especially if he has mastered them well. As your Mastery Review deck grows, this phase of instruction will take a bit longer, but should only take about 5-10 minutes if your child has mastered the phonemes and can respond quickly. In fact, my younger son used to like to see if he could go through all of the phonemes in less than a minute!

As you get toward the end of teaching and introducing new symbols, your teaching segment will become shorter and your Mastery Review segment will be longer, but not too much longer. Even with all of the phonemes in the deck, if your child has truly mastered them, it shouldn't take longer than 5-10 minutes to go through all of the phonemes.

When you have introduced every single phoneme, consider continuing with the Mastery Review each day for a period of time until your child can easily go through every phoneme and all of them consistently land in the "Know It" pile the first time through.

When you've introduced all of the phonemes, those introduced last will still take a bit of time for your child to reach automatic recall. Therefore, ongoing practice with the Mastery Review is a critical step in making sure your child truly has mastered all of the phonemes. We continued our daily Mastery Review deck drills for about four months after we had finished the Concentrated Practice for all of the phonemes.

When you have completed teaching all of the phonemes, you will need to implement daily one-on-one guided reading practice. At this point, you'll undertake a similar Introduction, Concentrated Practice, and Mastery Review for all of the sight words. You can work on one or two sight words integrated with your phonemes along the way, or you can begin practicing sight words following the phonemes.

No matter how you decide to handle your drill and practice sequences with both phonemes and sight words, you can see why it takes a long time and a lot of effort for your child to master reading.

When your remedial instruction is in full-swing, your total daily reading instruction time will be one and a half hours to two hours. Instruction will include:

1) ***About 30-45 minutes of direct sound-symbol, syllable, or sight word teaching and practice,***

2) ***About 20-30 minutes of guided reading practice,***

3) ***About 20-30 minutes of reading instruction through a multi-media program designed for the purpose of teaching reading skills.***

You may be wondering why you should you use an added multi-media program with all of the instruction you're providing. The primary reason is because research titled, "Computer-assisted instruction to prevent early reading difficulties in students at risk for dyslexia: Outcomes from two instructional approaches," by J. K. Torgesen, et al., 2010, shows a combination of direct teaching and computer-based multimedia practice provides the best educational outcomes for children with true dyslexia.

Additionally, teaching each phoneme and sight word to the point of mastery is time-consuming and tedious. The use of multimedia programs will help your child's learning progress faster, will add variation to the instruction, and add an element of fun, which makes it easier for you and your child.

In addition to working on the phonemes each day, you will eventually follow your 30-45 minute instructional period with side-by-side guided reading practice as will be discussed later in this book. The coming chapters will help you find programs and means for helping your child learn to read in less time. However, with true dyslexia, there is no quick fix, so set your mind on the long-term.

Start teaching your child the needed reading skills as soon as you can. Work with your child diligently and daily. One day your child will surprise you with his ability to read.

OFF THE SHELF OPTIONS

In the previous chapter, we talked about the Orton-Gillingham methodology for teaching children with dyslexia how to read. While you can implement the method using homemade materials, using a pre-packaged program can be a lot easier, especially if you haven't had O-G training. Scripted programs can be life-savers in terms of time and planning.

By "scripted," I mean the program tells you what to teach your child, when to teach it, and how to teach it. The program provides a foundational progression through the program that you can follow without having to track every phoneme, syllable, and sight word yourself.

Additionally, heavily scripted programs will tell you exactly what to say, provide teaching tips, and will provide you with guidance every step of the way. If you have no training in Orton-Gillingham or multisensory methods, and you have no desire to read "The Gillingham Manual," then a scripted program is likely to be easier for you to use. For that matter, a scripted program is easier for most people to use, but scripted programs can be expensive.

The primary benefit of using a pre-packaged program is that it is a handy, done-for-you solution. You can usually purchase all of the materials you need, you'll be given ideas for teaching activities, and sometimes the program even includes directions on what to say when teaching your child and may include all of the instructional materials you need.

Using a proven program is cheaper than paying a tutor by the hour to teach your child. As mentioned earlier, Renee Herman's research shows that remediation requires an hour or more of instruction every school day for three or more years to reach a proficient level of reading. Thus, the cost of having a tutor can add up significantly.

Additionally, practice needs to occur daily. For a typical 180 day school year, for three years, that would be 540 hours of instruction at one hour per day, which would equate to $13,500 dollars at $25 per hour. Great tutors cost more than that. Few of us can afford to pay a tutor to work with our child every day, but if you can, go for it!

Although you could try to go with one hour of tutoring per week, your child's progress will be comparable to the amount of one-on-one focused teaching he receives. In other words, it would take your child close to five times as long to become proficient at reading if he only receives one hour of tutoring per week. To bring forth more progress than once-per-week tutoring can provide, you can work with your child daily in addition to receiving tutoring. However, if you're working with your child every day, except on tutoring day, then you might as well tutor your child yourself.

Cost

The main drawback of using a do-it-yourself program is cost. Scripted programs are virtually always over $500 for the total, start-to-finish cost and programs range up to nearly $2000, depending upon which program you use. The main variables in cost are:

- The extent of teaching materials provided with the program, such as manipulatives, flashcards, books, etc.

- The level of scriptedness of the program (how much it provides in specific details of what to do and say each and every step along the way) and

- Whether the product is primarily built for use in a traditional school (more expensive, but more durable) or by home users.

Products targeted toward the school market tend to cost more because they will be used by multiple users and/or multiple students. Programs built primarily for single student use are often a lot cheaper.

Some pre-packaged programs can easily cost hundreds of dollars at each reading level. Nevertheless, using one of these programs is easier than trying to pull a program together, especially if you haven't had Orton-Gillingham training, and the programs are less expensive than ongoing tutoring for years to come.

Good program options for home instruction include:

- **ABeCeDanarian** – Initially targeted toward the home market, this program is an easy program to use, which parents seem to love. The practice reading materials have large lettering and widely spaced lines which helps children who may have additional visual-perception or ocular motor difficulties. The program itself is relatively straight-forward and is well-scripted so you know what to teach when and how to teach it. The program has four levels, A-D, for a comprehensive reading program.

- **All About Reading** – Written by Marie Rippel as a program to help her son after researching and learning all she could about teaching kids with dyslexia to read, this program is designed to be inexpensive and effective. Whether or not you choose to use AAR, they have a "Deluxe Reading

Kit" that is very reasonably priced. The kit is an excellent choice to use with other reading programs, particularly if you wish to teach your child without a specific program. AAR is designed for a parent to be the primary teacher. AAR teaches everything through sight, sound, and touch, and is very popular with homeschooling families because it is well-scripted, easy to use and understand, and it works well for most kids. The key to this program, as with all of them, is to be sure to stay with each phoneme to the point of mastery by your child.

- **Barton Reading And Spelling System** – This program was written by Susan Barton after she spent time helping her nephew overcome dyslexia. Susan trained in several different Orton-Gillingham based reading programs and realized there needed to be a simpler program, so she created one. The Barton Reading and Spelling System is designed specifically for a one-on-one tutorial model of teaching, so it is often a better fit than programs developed for the classroom environment. Many parents use and love the Barton Reading program. The most common complaint is the cost.

- **New Herman Method, The** – Renee Herman, a reading resource teacher, was personally helpful to me during the time I was learning about Orton-Gillingham based programs. The Herman Method is highly multisensory and ideal for students who are kinesthetic-tactile learners as opposed to more visual or auditory learners. The Herman Method incorporates visual, auditory, kinesthetic, and tactile modalities, so it really covers the bases well. The Herman Method is written primarily for the school market and Reading Resource rooms, but it is a well-scripted product that is viable for home users as well. The biggest issue with the New Herman Method is the pricing structure that provides multiple copies of the workbooks (assuming it will be used in the classroom). As such, it's expensive, but it is also a time-tested program that has existed for decades and has recently been updated to provide more efficient lessons.

- **S.P.I.R.E.** – (Specialized Program Individualizing Reading Excellence) – The S.P.I.R.E. program has been around for a couple of decades. This program was written by a teacher for the classroom environment but was introduced to me at my Orton-Gillingham Training Class for use by tutors. S.P.I.R.E. has been refined over the years, driven by research-proven outcomes, and is a highly refined solution for teaching reading to children with dyslexia. The system is comparable in cost to the Barton Reading and Spelling System with a per-level cost that adds up over multiple levels. The primary difference between this program and the others is the refinement of the program through ongoing research and the continual alignment with current best practices. S.P.I.R.E. is an excellent choice if you want to use the latest proven practices. S.P.I.R.E. is also an excellent resource for syllable type reading books for practice. They are also available as ebooks for iPad, etc.

- **Wilson Reading System** – Written by Barbara Wilson, the Wilson Reading System has been a mainstay in school reading resource programs, tutoring centers, and private schools for decades. This Orton-Gillingham based program is well-tailored to learners who are middle or high school students. The program was written in an era when reading disabilities were often not identified until a student was well past elementary reading instruction. Therefore, I think the Wilson Reading System is one of the better choices for a high school student who is beginning to receive remedial instruction. The Wilson Reading program is scripted and they offer training, which can be very helpful in understanding how to use the program. Unfortunately, the training is not available via online delivery at this time, so you'd have to find the nearest training opportunity to attend if you want to receive training. Information about training opportunities can be found on the Wilson website.

Each of these programs has been used by members of the Learning Abled Kids' support group and have been recommended by members who have used the programs. These programs have controlled studies proving each program's effectiveness.

There are other popular programs available. Some only have anecdotal stories of helping individual children, or they cite research that does not directly involve the use of their specific program.

For example, one program site I visited had a lot of research about multisensory teaching, explicit instruction, etc., but not one single study among those listed was a study of the use of their program as designed. It may be a fabulous program, but there is no way to know for sure unless the program is specifically studied to see if it is effective for children who have true, language-based dyslexia.

BE AWARE that not every program works well for every child. The success you and your child will have with any specific program will vary depending upon your diligence in using the program daily, the effectiveness of the instruction provided, whether the multi-sensory instruction being used meets your child's needs, and other factors.

Programs vary in the level of hands-on, kinesthetic, and visual instruction they incorporate into the instruction.

Therefore, if your child is highly kinesthetic or prefers hands-on learning, you may need to add multisensory activities to help your child learn from the program you select.

Also, the instructional quality, intensity, and the skills you personally bring into your child's lessons will provide varied degrees of learning success. If you cannot work well with your child, or do not work intensely with your child, then your child may not make meaningful progress.

It really helps to know yourself and to be realistic about whether you and your child can work with each other, or to consider whether you may need someone else to work with your child daily. Regardless of the program or the provider, daily instruction is needed for your child to make meaningful progress in learning to read.

Apps as Options

New on the reading remediation horizon, there are computer-based programs and apps that provide the Orton-Gillingham prescribed explicit and direct teaching. These apps will be easier to use in a lot of cases. However, many of the programs do not incorporate truly kinesthetic actions as part of the learning process.

Increasingly, apps are incorporating the use of touch screens, so they are more interactive than PC-based programs with point and click activities. If you have an iPad or Android tablet, and your child likes these devices, you might want to consider using an app for a portion of your instruction.

A caveat here is that these programs have not been heavily studied for their effectiveness yet. There are research studies showing apps on tablets can provide good learning outcomes, but no specific app emerges as a highly effective means of instruction (yet).

Therefore, although these apps are sometimes sold as

comprehensive solutions, I personally don't feel comfortable recommending an app as a stand-alone solution yet. I'm certain there will be some clear winners in the years ahead, so if this option appeals to you, check the ratings, research, and reviews for "phonemic awareness" and "Orton-Gillingham" apps regularly.

For now, I recommend using Orton-Gillingham based apps primarily for supplemental practice in addition to one of the above direct instruction reading programs. I'll cover some of the current market leaders in these types of apps when covering recommended practice programs.

One app for iPads, iPods, and iPhones that I wanted to mention is SoundLiteracy by 3D Literacy, LLC. This app has letter tiles and is designed to be a virtual solution to the letter-tile exercises in many Orton-Gillingham based programs. So if you'd prefer a virtual solution over physical letter tiles, and you own one of the Apple devices, this app may be a viable solution for O-G letter-tile exercises. The app lets your child take the tiles with him anywhere you go, which will allow your child to practice letter blending and segmenting skills wherever you are.

Please note: Sound Literacy is not an independent practice app. This app is designed to be used by a student in a side-by-side manner with a parent, tutor, or teacher. There is no auto-correct feature in the programming, so monitoring is required when working through the exercises. You'll want to be sure your child is saying the proper sound for each phoneme and is saying the sounds properly.

I'll cover more about this app and other apps in the "Practice, Practice, Practice" chapter that is upcoming. Apps are viable options for repetitive practice. For now, let's move into discussion of what to do if your child has significant phonemic awareness issues.

PHONEMIC AWARENESS DRILLS

Each Orton-Gillingham reading program teaches the phonemes directly, but some children need highly precise instruction in speaking and hearing the phonemes in order to understand them at the level required for reading. If you have a firm grasp on the sound-symbol correspondences and know precisely how to speak the phonemes, you can help your child with this skill. If not, you may need to hire a Speech-Language Pathologist (SLP) to help your child with this deeper level of phonemic instruction.

As it is with Orton-Gillingham based reading programs, teaching needs to be specific, detailed, and direct to make sure your child recognizes and pronounces each phoneme correctly. This skill is critical when your child begins to write and attempts to spell words based upon how he says the word or letter sound.

For example, if your child says the sound /r/ like the sound /w/, then she will have a difficult time sounding out and spelling words like rat, run, and race. Many kids speak words with r's in them using the sound /w/, but that doesn't necessarily mean the child has phonemic awareness difficulties. It may just be a speech impediment. Therefore, if your child has very few mispronounced words, she may just need a little bit of speech-language therapy to improve her articulation.

As another example, my son used to say "bebra" instead of zebra and "kapano" for piano. He had significant deficits in phonemic awareness and many mispronunciations. Needless to say, incorrect speaking of words leads to incorrect spellings. Thus, in order to read and write words properly, my son needed several years of speech-language services to learn to distinguish sounds precisely.

If your child has significant difficulty with phonemic awareness, you may need to work extra diligently to teach your child phonemic awareness skills. If a child has speech-language issues, is hard of hearing, or has an auditory processing disorder, she is much more likely to have difficulty articulating the precise phonemes represented by each sound-symbol. Children with these difficulties benefit from speech-language therapy if you can afford to provide it.

If you are going to work with your child at home, there are programs that will help you teach your child the needed preciseness. The biggest key is for you to be aware of and able to teach the very precise sound-symbol differences.

As an example, when you say the sounds /f/ and /v/, there is a difference in the pronunciation that is created by a slight shift in the air flow over your lips. A child cannot see the difference and can barely hear the difference, especially if he is not listening carefully. Explaining, showing, and teaching this slight sound shift requires skill!

As additional examples, the sounds /d/ and /t/ are similar as are /s/ and /z/, /k/ and /g/, /ch/ and /sh/, and so on. When you articulate those letters' sounds, you really don't vary the shape or position of your lips. The difference is in airflow and tongue placement. Some children need to be taught these differences carefully and explicitly.

To teach your child phonemic awareness, you will have to demonstrate with your lips, tongue placement and precise enunciation in order to help your child hear and speak the different sounds. Again, if you personally have difficulty with the sound represented by letters, it may be better to have a speech-language therapist work with your child.

If your child needs to receive speech-language instruction and detailed phonemic awareness training due to the severity of his reading disability, then the following two programs are the most likely to help your child develop phonemic awareness skills.

- **Lindamood-Bell LiPS** – LiPS is one of the best, industry standard programs you can buy for teaching a child phonemic awareness. One of the great aspects of this program is your ability to purchase the program and use it at home with your child over whatever length of time your child requires without additional tutoring expense.

  The LiPS program (Lindamood Phoneme Sequencing® Program) teaches each articulated sound using images and practice for the correct sound formation when listening and speaking. The precise understanding of each sound and the letters which represent the sound are taught through explicit hands-on instruction.

  The LiPS program is proven by research to be effective with a large number of children who have severe issues with dyslexia. The program is available for purchase through the Gander Publishing website, or you can hire a speech-language pathologist (SLP) who is trained to use the LiPS program.

  Hiring a provider is recommended if your child has severe articulation or phonemic awareness issues. We hired an SLP initially, which allowed me to observe the sessions through a one-way mirror.

  After observing the therapist working with my son for about a year, I was able to work with him using the LiPS methodologies at home. Having the ability to see the program in action made it easier for me to implement the LiPS techniques.

- **Fast Forword® and BrainPro®** – BrainPro is a computer-based version of the Fast ForWord program. You can use BrainPro with your child in a supported mode, with an online consultant. Alternately, you can go to a local provider for direct instruction using the Fast ForWord program. The programs are basically the same, so the primary difference will be whether you can work easily with your child using the BrainPro program and/or can't afford to pay a provider for the Fast ForWord program.

  Either way, Fast ForWord is an excellent program, but it does not let you work independently with your child without outside assistance. You must go to a provider or have an online consultant work with you. The primary reason for requiring a provider is to assure the quality and proper administration of the Fast ForWord or BrainPro programs. It is critical for your child to learn the phonemes the right way so she doesn't have to unlearn and relearn them if the instruction isn't properly provided. It is far more difficult for a child to relearn content than it is to learn it properly from the beginning.

  FastForword and BrainPro are proven programs with research showing their effectiveness. While you may pay more for either of these programs than other programs, having someone assist your child can be the best option. This is especially true if you and your child have difficulty working together on a regular basis or if you feel your child will benefit from a trained provider.

Both of the programs listed above are commonly used by speech-language therapists (SLPs). If you feel it would be better for your child to receive instruction from a trained SLP, you can call local SLPs to find one who understands phonemic awareness, works to improve phonemic skills, and who may use either LiPS or Fast ForWord.

Computer Based Practice

With the programs that follow, because a majority of the teaching is provided by a computer program, I will stress that you must monitor your child while she uses any of these programs. Observe carefully how your child says each phoneme.

A computer program cannot monitor with the same precision as a human observer, so you must sit with your child to be certain she is understanding each sound and speaking it correctly. Make immediate corrections when your child misspeaks a phoneme by pausing the program and having your child practice speaking the phoneme correctly. Precision is critical.

The programs will fail to provide the desired outcome for your child if you do not regularly monitor your child's use of the program to be sure she is articulating the sounds correctly. As mentioned before, it is more difficult to unlearn and relearn the phonemes than it is to teach them correctly the first time.

Computer Programs for Phonemic Awareness Practice:

• **Language Tune-Up Kit (LTK)** – This program has a built-in recording capability which is used to provide auditory feedback for your child. The LTK also provides direct instruction using an audio teaching feature. If your child needs integrated phonemic awareness instruction and an O-G reading program, the LTK is a great choice.

While the LTK is primarily a reading program, I am including it in the phonemic awareness section because the

LTK begins by systematically teaching each sound-symbol directly, using the built-in audio and recorded feedback. This makes it a good choice for phonemic awareness training. As a reading program, the LTK teaches more than 4400 words along with the phonemes in a logical sequence, building upon the phonemes your child has already learned.

While systematic instruction is precisely what is needed, the computer cannot always tell if your child is speaking each sound perfectly. Thus, I must caution again, if you use this program for teaching phonemic awareness, you must monitor your child as she speaks each sound to be certain she is articulating each sound properly.

If your child misspeaks a phoneme, make immediate corrections. Pause the program and having your child practice speaking the phoneme correctly. Monitoring your child's use of the program for preciseness and accuracy is essential for a good instructional outcome.

LTK includes a lot of student-based controls, which can be good or bad depending upon how prone your child is to making frequent adjustments to the pace of instruction, practice frequency, etc. Again, monitoring is beneficial.

▪ **Sound Reading** – Written specifically to help children with auditory processing problems, Sound Reading focuses on the precise phonemes that children need to know in order to read. The program is designed to work with clearly articulated sounds, so your child will be able to hear the differences in very similar phonemes.

Sound Reading also has what is called "Flash Fluency" built into the instruction. The fluency practice helps with reading mastery and is an excellent component of this program for enabling your child to become a proficient reader. This mastery focus is a critical component.

In several well-controlled studies, Sound Reading has been shown to bring forth excellent reading gains. The program is primarily designed to be used by a student as an independent learner. Because the sounds are strongly and precisely articulated in the instruction, you may not have to supervise your child as closely in the use of this program as you would the others, but some ongoing supervision is still recommended for your best results.

- **Earobics** – Earobics is an easy-to-implement solution you can use for teaching your child phonemic awareness skills at home. Earobics focuses on teaching phonological awareness and auditory processing skills. As with other programs, you will need to monitor your child's articulation of each sound as she uses the program.

Earobics monitors your child's ongoing recall of phonemes for mastery, adjusting your child's instruction as needed. Each time your child responds to an item, his mastery of the phoneme dictates whether or not he will be presented with additional practice of the phoneme on a time-delayed basis. This ongoing monitoring of mastery is critical for insuring that your child learns and retains each phoneme.

We used Earobics as part of our early phonemic awareness practice. When used in conjunction with LiPS, Earobics is a great way for your child to practice phonemic skills while using a program that is engaging to many kids.

The Earobics program is not a comprehensive reading program, but it is a comprehensive phonemic awareness practice program. It covers all of the phonemes but stops short of providing advanced reading instruction.

One additional caveat for this program: pay close attention to the required computer operating system for the version you are purchasing. Earobics was one of the earliest programs on the market designed for phonemic awareness practice. The advanced versions of the program have not been updated in several years. Thus, if you are on a Windows 7 or 8 platform, you may find an older version of the program does not work for you. There may be workarounds, but don't bank on them unless you are tech-savvy and have researched the matter first.

Earobics has been bought by Houghton-Mifflin and the Foundations Level is now offered inexpensively through Houghton-Mifflin as a single user product. I expect the more advanced levels may eventually be updated as well, but for now, you must be cautious about the version you buy. I'm hoping Houghton-Mifflin will update the entire program platform to function on newer operating systems soon.

- **Hear Builder Phonological Awareness** – As far as the recommended programs go, this is probably the most light-weight, and it is best suited for teaching mid-level phonemic awareness skills. Hear Builder focuses more on segmenting and blending skills than it does on precise teaching of the phonemes themselves, so this would be a good program to use as a follow-up to Earobics.

If your child knows the basic phonemes, but struggles with sounding out words or spelling, the Hear Builder program would be a wise choice as a skill building program. If your child still needs to work on phonological skills, you'll want to work with a program like Earobics first.

Given your child has significant phonemic awareness issues, I'd recommend having your child work with a phonemic awareness program (or two) prior to working on advanced reading skills. After your child has completed programs like Earobics and Hear Builder, then you can move into a comprehensive O-G reading program, knowing your child has good mastery of phonemic awareness.

To sum up this chapter, if your child needs to work on phonemic awareness skills, have your child complete a phonemic awareness program before beginning Orton-Gillingham-based reading instruction. If your child needs to use a cognitive enhancement program, you can provide that program simultaneously with either a phonemic awareness program or an O-G program.

If your child is in public school, you'll probably need to use one program followed by another to avoid overwhelming your child with homework and extra cognitive work. If you are homeschooling, you can use a cognitive enhancement program in addition to phonemic awareness or O-G instruction as part of your child's typical school day.

Regardless of which program(s) you choose, your child will need to use a practice program on a daily basis. Ideally, the practice program would be used 20 to 30 minutes just prior to bed. Compliance may be easier to manage if you let your child have a break after school anyway.

Why before bed? It has been shown that activity undertaken right before sleep allows the brain to continue processing the information while a person is sleeping. Thus, using the program just prior to bed will enable more of the phonemic instruction to remain in your child's mind. This could bring about better mastery of the phonemes in a shorter period of time.

Next up, we'll talk more about other types of programs you may use for reading practice. This chapter and the previous one discuss foundational reading skills, but there are several phases of reading remediation. The next three chapters discuss acquisition of reading proficiency through more advanced skill building.

PRACTICE, PRACTICE, PRACTICE

If you want your child to truly be successful and to retain the phonemic awareness skills he is learning, it is important for your child to practice regularly using a computer-based program. Undertaking daily practice on a computer, whether you teach your child through direct lessons or not, will help solidify your child's reading skills and enable him to become a more fluent reader.

During the week, if you have your child practice with a computer program like Lexia, Language Tune-UpKit, etc., on a daily basis, the extra practice will keep him moving forward. Using a program for 20-30 minutes before bed as part of a bedtime routine is ideal.

You may wonder if you really need to use both a face-to-face Orton-Gillingham program and a computer-based practice program. Research shows using both types of programs will provide better results for your child.

In a study published in the "Annals of Dyslexia; 2010" (Vol 60, Issue 1) titled "Computer-assisted instruction to prevent early reading difficulties in students at risk for dyslexia: Outcomes from two instructional approaches," the research found a combination of direct instruction and computer-based programs was more effective than either teaching model by itself (Torgesen, J. K., et al., 2010). The difference in learning progress across the control groups was significant, so it is wise for you to provide your child with both computer-based and person-to-person instruction.

I believe the use of a computer program in addition to person-to-person teaching helps because the computer programs provide comprehensive practice. Computers don't skip steps, forget phonemes, or overlook anything. By nature, if the program is thoroughly written, it will teach your child every phoneme he needs to know. At a minimum, a computer program will ensure no instructional gaps exist.

When I began helping my son overcome his dyslexia, we used a dual instruction approach. It was a highly effective combination for us. We used homemade materials, the teaching sequence I learned in my Orton-Gillingham training, along with Earobics, Simon Sounds It Out, and Lexia Learning's reading software programs to provide a comprehensive reading instruction program for my son.

During our three years of intense remediation, my son had one-on-one instruction with me followed by practice with one of the software programs. The third period of time within our reading instruction involved side-by-side, guided reading practice which you'll learn about in another chapter.

Providing remedial instruction through a traditional Orton-Gillingham reading program, used in combination with an Orton-Gillingham-based computer program, is a proven combination. I truly believe every parent who wants to enable her child to make adequate yearly progress should provide instruction via both methods until her child can read well.

If your child is attending a traditional school and receiving daily reading instruction at school, and given that instruction is adequate, you may be able to simply add daily practice with a computer-based reading program to your child's day. If your child is homeschooled, you can provide both face-to-face and computer-based practice as part of your regular school programming.

One of the reasons I pay close attention to the research results for the programs or methods I suggest is to ensure the programs and methods are effective, at least for a number of students. I do not want you to end up wasting your child's time with ineffective programs. However, whether a specific program or method will be effective for your child depends upon the way you implement the program and whether the program fills the specific needs your child has in his learning struggles. Also, I highly recommend you look for the latest news and research on any given program before using it just in case there have been changes to the program and/or there are new, important research outcomes.

Using an Orton-Gillingham instructional program, a computer-based practice program, and engaging in guided reading practice on a daily basis are the keys to accelerating your child's reading progress. Guided reading practice, as we will discuss in the next chapter, will help your child use the skills he is learning through whatever forms of instruction he is receiving. Side-by-side reading practice will help solidify the phoneme skills your child has learned.

For best results, any reading, writing, and spelling programs you choose should include both audio and visual teaching. The teaching portion of the programs you choose must provide comprehensive, explicit, direct instruction using a sequence of skill building.

As a reminder: be certain the program you choose teaches the sound represented by each phoneme, and focuses on the sound a letter represents rather than the letter's name. For example, you do NOT want the program to show the symbol "b" and then say "bee" because the letter "b" represents the sound /b/ as in bubble. You want the program to show the symbol "b" and provide the sound /b/ when you read, which is an ever so brief "buh" sound.

Comprehensive Reading Skills Programs

Two comprehensive, Orton-Gillingham based software programs I prefer for reinforced learning of reading skills are Lexia Reading and Language Tune-Up Kit. Each of these two programs provides instruction from beginning reading skills to levels beyond sixth grade reading abilities.

Lexia Reading (http://lexialearning.com/) – There are two levels within the Lexia Reading program family: Lexia Core5 ® is for students from Preschool to 5th grade, Strategies for Older Students (SOS) is for 6th grade through adult. The Lexia programs start by teaching the phonemes then provide advanced reading instruction, including providing reading comprehension instruction. They cover each level of reading decoding skill that is required to take a student from a non-reader to a proficient reader.

Our heavy-duty, computer-based reading instruction began with Lexia's Strategies for Older Students (SOS) program. My boys were in third and fifth grade at the time. Both of my boys really liked the SOS program, so we never had any issues with instructional compliance.

Strategies for Older Students was perfect for my fifth grader. He had complained of another program being "too little kiddish," so I opted for Lexia's SOS program, which foregoes cartoonish graphics in favor of a straight-forward, uncluttered, and sophisticated instructional presentation.

However, I want to warn you: This program has been modified and updated for Common Core and now includes timed elements that reduce some kids with slow processing speeds to tears. I've received reports from several parents stating that Lexia is highly frustrating and "impossible" for their child to successfully complete due to a slow processing speed. Therefore, if your child has a slow processing speed, you might want to choose one of the other programs.

The levels within the Lexia programs cover

phonological awareness, word attack skills, Greek and Latin roots, and more. The Lexia program has been part of countless research studies through the years and is proven to be an effective instructional platform for teaching reading skills to students who have true dyslexia.

Language Tune-Up Kit (http://www.jwor.com) – The LTK is not an online program, but it is a computer-based program you load onto your computer via CD-Roms or direct download. The LTK is designed to provide an entire reading program that will enable a child to read up to an 8.5 grade level. The LTK also includes a card deck and a placement test to help you determine which lesson you should begin with when teaching your child. JWor Enterprises will provide you with a free demo CD-rom if you request one from them.

Beginning Skills Reinforcement (Incomplete Programs)

The following programs are recommended for practice with an elementary aged child who needs to begin with the most basic reading skills. You would use these programs for fun practice through to completion, then follow the program with Lexia Reading or the LTK through to completion for a comprehensive approach to reading skill practice, depending upon your child's processing speed.

Funnix Reading (http://funnix.com/) – Funnix is an incremental progression program with copious amounts of skill review. Their website says the program introduces approximately 10% new material with each lesson, so 90% of the lesson will be review for your child.

Progression is step-by-step to ensure your child does not feel overwhelmed. If your child has memory-related learning difficulties, then Funnix might be a good choice because of the incremental progress and constant review.

The program also uses story-based lessons, so that can also help make connections for kids who have a stronger narrative learning style. This program currently takes a child through a second grade reading level, so follow-up with a more advanced reading skills program, like Lexia or LTK, is required for your child to develop reading proficiency.

Reading Eggs (http://readingeggs.com/) – Reading Eggs is being used by schools as a "Response to Intervention" type of program. The program is not specifically an Orton-Gillingham based program for remediating learning disabilities, but it is an engaging, interactive program your child can use and is likely to benefit from.

Reading Eggs currently begins with the earliest elements of reading instruction and works at a progression that takes a child to a grade 2 reading level. Reading Eggs may be more fun as a beginning program for your child if he's in elementary school.

As with Funnix, Reading Eggs is not a comprehensive reading program, so you'll need to follow Reading Eggs with a more sophisticated program, like Lexia Reading or LTK. Before purchasing, be sure to take advantage of their free trial to see if the program will be suitable for your child.

Earobics – Earobics, as discussed in the prior chapter, is also a viable beginning reading practice program. Even though it is geared more toward children who have phonemic awareness or auditory processing problems, the program is solid for teaching early reading skills.

To reiterate my prior caveat for this program, pay close attention to the required computer operating system for running the Earobics program. As an older program, you may find Earobics will not run on your computer.

Also, currently you can't purchase Earobics directly from the publisher for home use. However, you can purchase the program for home use through Christianbook.com. It is not a "Christian" program, and I'm not sure why Christianbook is the only retailer I can find for Earobics, but don't let the seller's name stop you from purchasing the program. It is a great program.

We used the program with our boys and they both liked it. The program is both easy and effective to use.

Practice Apps

If you have a touch screen enabled tablet, your child might really like using an app on a tablet for practice. While using a laptop or desktop is certainly viable, there is added interactivity with a tablet-based app that your child won't get from clicking a mouse. The previously listed programs work well as reinforcement learning activities since they are thorough, but they are not overly tactile or kinesthetic.

I will point out a few apps here that I feel would be good apps for practice, but I'm going to reserve providing robust information about apps since research data proving the effectiveness of these apps isn't overly available yet. While the research is still out on apps, I suspect research data documenting the effectiveness of apps for reading remediation will be published in the near future.

If your child is a highly kinesthetic or tactile learner, you may find these apps work particularly well for your child. For children with highly kinesthetic learning styles, activity-based learning is extremely important. Therefore, it's important to be conscious of how much tactile, hands-on, and large body movement-based learning your child is receiving during his reading instruction. Using a hands-on app may mean a world of difference for your child if he is a kinesthetic learner.

Since there are new apps being produced every day, please go searching for apps in Android app stores or in the iTunes store. If your tablet is an Android tablet, you can find a large number of apps on Amazon.com. Your keywords in searching should be: Orton-Gillingham, phonemic awareness, and multisensory.

As I present each of the apps that follow, I'll let you know whether the app covers beginning skills, mid-level skills, is a complete program, or if the program provides less comprehensive supplemental practice.

Apps for Android Devices

Doodling Dragons by Pedia Learning Inc. – This is a beginning phonemic awareness app which teaches each sound represented by each letter. If a letter represents multiple sounds, like the vowels have both short and long sounds, then the app teaches both sounds in combination with the letters. Parents in the Learning Abled Kids' support group say their kids love this app, so that is always a positive factor. If a child loves an app, then he is much more likely to use the app regularly for practice.

Montessori Words & Phonics for Kids by L'Escapadou – This app is very similar to Doodling Dragons because it also teaches beginning reading skills. The description uses the term Phonics for the teaching, but it is truly a phonemic awareness program. The program teaches a child to hear, recognize, and use the sound-symbol phonemes as a foundation for reading skills. This program has been around a little bit longer than Doodling Dragons and has very positive feedback on its use and results.

There are other apps as well, and you may certainly choose one of them if it sounds like your child will benefit from that app. The apps listed here are not endorsed by me at all, since I've not actually used them, but they are provided as information to you about apps that are available and may be worthwhile for your child to use for practice.

Apps for iPad <u>or</u> iPod (Apple)

Phonics With Phonograms by Logic of English – As a phonemic awareness practice program, I love Logic of English's straightforward lessons. Phonics with Phonograms is designed to teach the most prevalent 74 phonograms to the point of mastery. The app's design is both sophisticated and simple, which makes it functional for young children, teens, and even adults. There are no cartoonish, babyish graphics or characters in this app. Therefore, if you have a middle schooler or a teenager who needs to begin practice with simple list phonemic awareness skills, then I would highly recommend this app as an excellent choice.

Logic of English is not, however, a comprehensive reading practice program. It is limited to teaching phonemic awareness skills for the 74 most common phonemes. The program does not teach syllabication, word blending and segmenting, and other advanced reading skills at the time I am writing this book.

Therefore, this program is an excellent choice for any child with significant phonemic awareness difficulties and should be used until all of the phonemes are mastered. Once these 74 phonemes are mastered, then you would want to use a practice program or app that will teach your child more advanced reading skills.

abc PocketPhonics: letter sounds & writing + first words by My Pocket Ltd – I love this app because it allows your child to trace the letters and teaches the letter sounds, not the letter names. When it comes to solid Orton-Gillingham practices, teaching the sounds represented by letters and letter combinations is essential. This program, through the letter tracing, also allows a student to work on writing skills.

Children are also taught sound blending skills to form words, so this is a very well-rounded app for enabling your child to practice phonemic awareness skills. Perhaps best of all, the app also provides progress reports online when a parent registers the app. As you are working with your child, this reporting can be valuable as a tool to help you know what skills your child is practicing with the app.

OG Card Deck by Mayerson Academy – the OG Card Deck is similar to the Logic of English app previously mentioned. The OG Card Deck reviews 80 of the most common phonemes.

This app differs from the Logic of English app because it provides short video clips demonstrating the proper articulation of each phoneme. These video clips would be especially beneficial for children who have speech-language or auditory processing difficulties. Learning how to properly speak the phonemes is essential when the child attempts to spell words by sounding them out.

Also similar to the Logic of English app, this app is not a comprehensive reading skills program. While it does include consonant digraphs, vowel combinations, and common suffixes, it does not advance into word attack skills needed to read or spell multi-syllable words.

Therefore, once again, this program should be used until your child masters the 80 phonemes taught in the app. When your child has mastered the skills within this app, then you would need to select a program or app to help your child practice advanced reading skills.

Simplex Spelling Phonics - Rhyming With CVC Words by Pyxwise Software Inc. – the Simplex Spelling Phonics app is unique because it is an intermediate skill program. This program teaches 300+ consonant – vowel – constant (or CVC) three letter words that are common in the English language.

As a child types a letter for a word, the app speaks the sound represented by the letter. Using the phonemic sounds is an essential component for your child to understand the sound-symbol correlations.

I refer to this program as an intermediate skill program because it does not teach the sound-symbol correlations as independent lessons. Although the program heavily incorporates the sound-symbol correlations, it does not teach them directly and explicitly as is required by some children. Therefore, this app is not a comprehensive reading remediation program.

If your child has extreme difficulty with phonemic awareness, it may be highly beneficial for your child to practice with one of the apps that teaches the most common phonemes directly such as the Logic of English app or the OG Card Deck, and then use this Simplex Spelling Phonics app as the next practice program. After your child has mastered the 300 CVC words in Simplex Spelling Phonics, you could move to a program or app designed to teach advanced word attack skills.

Apps for iPad (Apple)

Learn to Read, Write and Spell by Rogers Center for Learning – This program is designed to be a comprehensive remediation program based upon Orton-Gillingham practices. The program is designed to advance a child from a non-reader to a sixth grade reading level. The program is designed to teach everything from phonemes to blending and segmenting, spelling skills, prefixes and suffixes, and much more.

The program includes progress reporting as well as the ability to select individual lessons. This feature can be beneficial if you would like to select the specific skill you would like for your child to practice in relation to the hands-on Orton-Gillingham lessons you are currently studying.

As a comprehensive reading remediation program, this app would be an excellent choice. I'll be excitedly looking forward to research being published to see whether this app works effectively as a standalone, Orton-Gillingham based reading program.

SoundLiteracy by 3D Literacy, LLC – Please note: Sound Literacy is not an independent practice app. This app is designed to be used by a student in a side-by-side manner with a parent, tutor, or teacher. There is no auto-correct feature in the programming, so a teacher is required to monitor and walk through the exercises with the student to be sure the student is saying the sounds properly.

The program has letter tiles and is designed to be a virtual solution to the letter-tile exercises in Orton-Gillingham based programs. Rather than having letter tiles lying all over the place, or worrying about losing letters, the program lets you take virtual tiles with you wherever you go. The portability allows your child to practice letter blending and segmenting skills anytime, anywhere.

Although I have provided information about several programs and apps you can use for your child's reading skill practice, please don't consider this list complete. There are new programs and apps being developed even as I write, and there are many viable programs available.

If you don't see the solution your child needs, please search out other programs that you feel would better suit your child's specific needs. When searching, just be sure to pay close attention to whether the program teaches phonemes rather than the letter names.

Also, you may want to take note as to whether the program or app specifically states that it teaches phonemic awareness skills and/or whether the programming is based upon Orton-Gillingham's best practices. If the program you choose teaches phonemic awareness skills, and uses multisensory instruction or Orton-Gillingham based methods, then it is likely your child will benefit from the program.

As a matter of consumer savviness, be sure to note whether any cited research is proving the effectiveness of the actual program, or whether the research documents the effectiveness of a particular method. For example, I've seen retailers say, "Direct instruction is proven to work," and they cite research. However, they don't have any research that proves their instruction or program is effective.

In fact, I've seen sites with research statements and reports offered as "proof" all over their website, but the controlled studies did not pertain to the publisher's actual product. They had testimonies and anecdotal stories too, but individual cases do not prove the effectiveness of a program.

As discussed in the introduction to this book, also be alert to whether a program is designed for the specific need your child has, or whether the marketer is selling his program based upon the definition of dyslexia rather than the diagnosis. It can be difficult to sort it all out, but I do hope this book gives you more clarity in your decision making.

A Review of Practice Protocols

In case you are feeling a bit overwhelmed, I thought I'd offer a clear summary of what we've covered so far. If your child has been diagnosed with dyslexia by a qualified neuropsychologist or educational psychologist, then your child needs phonemic awareness instruction.

To provide the needed instruction, use these guidelines:

1) If your child has severe phonemic awareness problems, especially when accompanied by speech-language or auditory processing difficulties, begin with one of the Phonemic Awareness Programs. Provide both face-to-face instruction and computer-based practice until your child masters the basic phonemes.

2) When your child has mastered the basic phonemes, or if your child does not need intensive phonemic awareness instruction, then you can proceed with a traditional Orton-Gillingham program and a computer-based practice on a daily basis.

If your child's school is providing adequate face-to-face instruction, then you can simply use an appropriate O-G practice program to reinforce the skills your child is learning during the day. Have your child use this program as part of his bedtime routine if possible.

3) Begin guided reading practice as part of your evening routine (reading together) when your child is able to decode simple one or two syllable words. If appropriate, you can use guided reading practice while helping your child complete any reading that is part of his regular school work. Guided Reading is explained in the next chapter.

In the chapters following the "Guided Reading Practice" chapter, we will discuss advanced reading skills, writing issues, and spelling as areas typically affected by true dyslexia.

I'm proud of you for hanging in here because I know sorting dyslexia and its remediation out can feel overwhelming. Having been there and having gone through this myself, I hope to make things easier for you and your child.

GUIDED READING PRACTICE

One of the most important activities you can undertake to help solidify your child's reading skills is Side-by-Side Reading. Whether your child is in a reading program at school or homeschooled, your child needs lots and lots of practice using his newly learned decoding skills in order to become a skilled reader.

When considering all of the remediation activities we undertook, side-by-side reading was by far the most enjoyable. Side-by-side reading creates a great bond with your child if you approach the activity as though you are a compassionate reading coach. This is your opportunity to carefully walk your child through each step in decoding words as he reads. Enjoy this time with your child.

Grab a great book that is at your child's current reading level. If it's winter, get yourself a big cozy blanket and curl up on the couch with your child. If it's summertime, pack a picnic lunch, a blanket, and go to a park, the beach, or your backyard. Don't race through the book.

Enjoy the side-by-side reading with your child. Your child will grow so quickly. Relish this phase of your reading remediation program because it won't last long and your child will soon want to read independently.

Selecting Books to Read

One of the most critical steps in beginning to use side-by-side reading is the selection of appropriate reading material. In order for your child to be successful with and not frustrated by side-by-side reading, you need to select books that are at an appropriate interest level (IL) and reading level (RL) for your child.

Selecting appropriate books can be a challenge with remedial readers because the books that are easy to read are often well below the child's intellectual interests for his age. However, there are books called Hi–Lo books which are written to appeal to a variety of interest and reading levels.

Basically, Hi-Lo books have topics of interest to older children but a reading level that is quite a bit lower than the child's age or grade level. Using High–Lo books will engage your child in reading better than using books with topics that are too elementary in nature for your child.

Select Hi–Lo books based upon your child's interest level (IL) and reading level (RL). Choose books with an interest level (IL) close to your child's current cognitive understanding or grade level and with a reading grade level (RL) close to your child's current level of reading ability.

For example, if your child is in sixth grade, but reads on a second grade level, then you would want to purchase books that have a rating of IL=6, RL=2. That's a grade 6 interest level and a grade 2 reading level.

In another example, say your child is in eighth grade, but cognitively your child understands concepts around a fifth grade level and reads on a third grade level. You would want to select books with an IL=5, RL=3 rating.

The key is to select books that will be of interest to your child but have a reading level that is not too difficult. You don't want reading practice to be discouraging. Neither do you want to select books where the reading level is so easy that your child isn't advancing in his reading skills. You want to pick books that are ever so slightly above your child's current level of reading mastery.

Pick books with a reading level that is .5 or 1 grade level above your child's current reading level. Don't try to jump into higher level reading, or you will frustrate your child's attempts at decoding the words. At times, when it's been awhile since your child's last testing, you may have to make an educated guess about your child's current reading level, but hopefully that won't be too difficult if you've been purchasing reading materials with increasingly advanced content.

You can find good Hi–Lo books through several specialty publishers. You can also buy mass-market traditional books, given you pay attention to the reading level contained within the book. I'll list a few publishers that you may want to use for selecting books for your child, but I'd like to offer a suggestion first.

When selecting books for your child to use in side-by-side reading practice, it is often highly beneficial to carefully select nonfiction or classic literature books based upon your child's current academic studies. Using carefully chosen books will help your child by providing extra content review for topics he needs to know.

If your child is in public school, select books related to topics your child is currently studying or will be studying soon. Side-by-side reading practice using carefully chosen books will benefit your child by helping him learn content he needs to know for his regular schooling without spending a lot of extra time studying in addition to working on reading. You can also use his regular school books for reading practice when your child is within 1-2 grade levels of the needed reading skill level.

If your child is homeschooled, you can efficiently cover classic literature, science, and social studies topics by using carefully chosen books for your reading practice. The benefit in using Hi-Lo books related to the school subjects your child needs to know otherwise is that your homeschool day will be shortened. When you are spending up to two hours per day working on reading skills, I think it is easy to see how the use of carefully chosen Hi-Lo books for reading practice will make your school day more efficient.

That said, the following are specialty providers of reading materials for children who need Hi-Lo books. Search on each publisher's website for Hi-Lo and you should be able to find a variety of books to choose from.

Specialty Hi-Lo Book Publishers

Please be advised, this is not a comprehensive list of all Hi-Lo publishers, and an increasing number of publishers are providing Hi-Lo books. If you do not find books of interest to your child with these providers, please search other booksellers, Amazon, and the Internet for additional providers of Hi-Lo reading books.

One of the easiest places to begin your search for Hi-Lo books is on Amazon.com because they carry books from a wide variety of publishers, including some of the publishers listed below. Simply go to Amazon and search for "Hi-Lo reading books."

Several of the publishers below have narrow-niche specialties, so if your child fits in the niche for that publisher, you're likely to be able to quickly and easily find books to meet your needs with those publishers.

Wieser Educational Resources for Struggling Learners – Wieser is focused on educational publishing. They have a *wide variety of non-fiction books* you can use for efficient reading practice while studying science, social studies, history, etc. Wieser has a simple search method—just check the boxes at the top of their webpage for your child's Interest Level and Reading Level and press "search."

You'll easily locate books suitable for your child's reading needs. As far as non-fiction Hi-Lo book providers go, I love Wieser for their wide selection and easy-to-search selections. Wieser is a great provider for homeschooling parents to use in finding books to serve both general curriculum needs and your child's reading practice needs.

Bearport Publishing provides books specifically targeted to children with a ***Middle School Interest level***. Hi-Lo books for reluctant readers are provided at a variety of reading levels below the middle school level, but with topics and concepts suitable for children in middle school. Thus, if you have a child in middle school, Bearport may be your quickest and easiest resource for Hi-Lo books of interest to your child.

Bright Apple has unique products designed to improve the basic skills of students with special needs as well as those performing below grade level. They have Hi-Lo books about a wide variety of topics. They also offer games, teaching/learning tools and more.

Capstone Classroom is a great source for *social studies and science* books with a lower reading level. You can use their "Leveling Tool" to obtain a list of the books that fit your child's specific needs. This tool can really help cut down on the time you spend searching for books that meet your needs.

High Noon Books provides appropriately formatted independent readers for students in ***upper elementary and junior high***. They have low-level readers a student can carry around without being embarrassed. The books are designed with extra sight word practice and are specifically written to exercise a child's reading skills.

Perfection Learning is the publisher of the Accelerated Reading program. They provide an extensive line of Hi/Lo books for reluctant readers, including popular series like "Passages" by best-selling author Anne Schraff; the Retold line of classic novels, short stories, myths and folktales; and Cover-to-Cover chapter books, informational books, novels, and timeless classics. Simply look on their main menu for the High Interest / Low Reading entry.

Pro•ed offers a wide variety of learning products for special education, gifted education, and developmental disabilities. Look in PRO-ED, Inc.'s "Literature and Hi-Lo Readers" section within their Literacy section to find their line of "Adapted Classics" and other books. The "Adapted Classics" are an excellent choice for exposing your child to classic literature at a reading level he can manage. These books can expose your child to the same classic literature other students his age are reading, which helps your child stay "on track" with his content-based learning.

Remedia Publications has Interest Level and Reading Level specified as the first elements in each book's description, so they don't have a search option for "Hi-Lo" books. Remedia's books are created with struggling students in mind, so they focus on the essential skills that are needed to master reading. The content is presented in sequential steps with short exercises, repetition, format variety, with simple, non-distracting art.

Sundance Publishing provides research-based instruction in their Hi-Lo books. They have been publishing for years and have thousands of leveled reading books on a wide variety of topics to choose from. Their books are classified as "Reading for below-level readers," so look in that category within the middle school and high school tabs for books that may be of interest to your child.

Side-by-Side Reading Tools

When you are practicing side-by-side reading, you will find it easier to work with your child if you have an index card, reading guide, pencil or pointing implement in hand.

You won't need an index card AND a reading guide, but you will find it beneficial to have an index card OR a reading guide. Perhaps you'd like a reading guide made out of an index card!

What is a reading guide, you ask? A reading guide is usually a piece of cardstock, laminated card, or strip of plastic with a rectangular cut-out or a clear see-through window. The cut-out / window is often the height of one line of printed text so the guide can be moved as your child reads. The window only reveals one word, one sentence, or a few sentences at a time, depending on the size of the cutout reading window.

The benefit of using a reading guide is that it helps your child keep his place while reading, and the window keeps your child focused on the specific words he is supposed to read. Children who have any sort of visual processing, visual-perception, or ocular motor difficulties often benefit from having a reading guide to help them focus on one word or sentence at a time.

Children with true dyslexia may feel overwhelmed with the thought of having to read all the words on a page. Having a limited number of words visible can help your child focus on only one or a few words at a time, which makes the number of words feel less overwhelming.

Reading guides can be purchased online via Amazon.com by searching for "reading guide." Some call them "reading windows" or "reading strips," but they are all basically the same thing. You can make a reading guide by cutting a $1/8^{th}$ or $1/4^{th}$ inch slit in a blank, unlined index card that is at least an inch long, but up to four inches long. I prefer to use a 5x7 index card because it will cover more of the page as your child is reading. 3x5 cards are too small for large books, so a 5x7 card is more versatile.

One Learning Abled Kids' mom shares that she simply cuts off the upper left-hand corner of an index card. When reading, they place the card where the snipped corner reveals one syllable at a time as they slide the card to the right. It helps when first learning to sound out words. For example, if the word is "letter," they can slide the card to reveal "let" and then "ter." Using the snipped-corner card is an easy-to-use variation of a standard reading guide.

If your child only needs mild guidance and you don't need to limit the exposure of the other text on the book's page, then you may find an index card works well to cover the text either above or below where your child is currently reading. Simply slide the index card, or a blank strip of paper, down the page as your child reads to help him stay on the proper line.

It's important to use a plain card, not a brightly colored card. You can use a strip of paper in a pastel color or plain white paper if you prefer paper. You don't want your reading guide to have any writing or a design that will be distracting to your child visually as he tries to read. You can even let your child pick his own color for his card as a way of giving him a bit of perceived control over his schooling.

For our guided reading practice, we simply used an index card with the blank side facing up. We used our card to underline the sentence currently being read. However, it is a better practice to cover the text your child just read, so the card is above the text currently being read. Having the card above the text, and moving the card downward over the text your child has already read, can help your child easily sweep to the next line of text when he reaches the end of each line.

If your card is below the line currently being read, you or your child has to move the reading guide down before your child can start reading the next line. I think having the card come down and cover the just-read text allows for more fluent reading, especially as your child's reading skills advance to a point where he reads quickly and no longer wants to use a reading guide.

The other tool you'll need for helping your child through side-by-side reading is a pencil, pen, stylus, or some other pointing implement. A mechanical pencil, retracted ballpoint pen, or a stylus pointer are the best tools to use.

You can use a standard pencil when you have a book you are able to write in. Being able to write in the book is the most helpful in terms of helping your child learn how to decode multi-syllable words. If you can start with books that you are free to write in with a regular pencil, then you can teach your child the precise division of words.

Your pointing implement is used to point to the divisions between syllables as your child tries to figure out where to split the word in order to read it. When your child doesn't know where to split a word, you can use a scooping mark or a slash mark between syllables. "Scooping" is when you use a curved line (an arc) underneath or above a word in order to show the separate syllables. A slash is simply a line drawn as a separator between syllables. We'll talk about these methods in the next section of this chapter.

When you've acquired appropriate books, some sort of reading guide, and a pointing implement, you are ready to begin side-by-side reading practice with your child. You can use the side-by-side guided reading whenever you read with your child—whether your child is doing the reading or you are reading aloud. Similarly, you can hold and move the reading guide in the beginning, but your child should learn to use the reading guide too.

How To Use The Side-by-Side Reading Method

Did I tell you how much I love side-by-side reading? I remember our cozy winter days, cuddled up on the sofa with a great book, practicing reading together. In side-by-side reading, your child does not do all of the reading. You read aloud too, so you can demonstrate fluent reading skills for your child.

In the beginning of your side-by-side reading practice, alternate turns with your child. Start by reading a sentence yourself, using the guided reading protocol, then have your child read a sentence, then you read a sentence, then have your child read a sentence, and so on.

After a few weeks of reading practice alternating sentence by sentence, switch to alternating paragraph by paragraph. After a few more weeks, switch to alternating pages of reading—one page read by you, one page read by your child. When reading a full page is comfortable for your child, move to reading two pages each, then three pages each, etc.

Ultimately, you'll end up reading a chapter and your child will read a chapter, but only one chapter each per day. Eventually, your child will reach a point where he would rather read the book by himself. When you reach that point, have your child read one chapter aloud, then he can read the second chapter silently. You will want to verify that your child can tell you what happened in the chapter before you permit him to read completely on his own.

With the side-by-side reading protocol, you will use your reading guide to track the words or sentences as you or your child reads. Using a reading guide helps your child easily maintain his place as reading moves forward.

Scientifically, a child can read much faster if his eyes are not searching for the beginning of the proper line each time his eyes sweep back to the left-hand side of the page. Therefore, the reading guide helps your child develop a more fluent reading pace, which is a great skill to develop in any child.

It's also noteworthy that many speed reading programs recommend using a finger moving down the left-hand side of the page to maintain the reading place and pace as readers move down the page. While we're not trying to create speed readers here, using a reading guide, a pointer, or your finger does provide your child with a smoother reading pace.

The second part of the side-by-side reading protocol involves using your pointer whenever your child reaches a multi-syllable word he has difficulty decoding. Use your pencil or pointer to segment the word for your child. If you can write in the book, your markings will look similar to this, depending upon the method you're using:

The image shows how your markings will look if you're marking from the top, the bottom, or using slashes. How you mark the syllables will depend on whether you are using your reading guide above, below, or over the text. Generally speaking, you will use scoops when you are moving an index card down the page. You can use slashes whether you are marking through the window in your reading guide or moving an index card down the page.

Adding diacritical marks such as the long vowel *mark* (‾), *called* the macron, over long vowel sounds and a breve (˘) over short vowels can help your child with decoding. You can cross out silent letters too, if it helps your child.

If you are using a book you cannot mark in, use your pointer to indicate where the syllable divisions occur. You or your child can point to each word as your child reads.

Have your child try to sound out the individual syllables before providing assistance but don't hesitate too long or your child will become tired and frustrated.

Remember, syllable division is difficult for your child, so he will benefit from encouragement and positive feedback. Say, "GREAT JOB!" whenever he independently decodes a complex word.

As your child tries to sound out the individual syllables, coach him by calmly asking him about the phonemes within the syllable. For example, if the word is baseball, you can ask him how the "e" changes the sound of the "a" in the first syllable (base). Then you can ask him to sound out "ball."

Use your Orton-Gillingham knowledge to dissect each word. Prompt your child by saying the represented sounds if needed. Help your child decipher each word phoneme-by-phoneme and syllable-by-syllable.

If the book's reading level is well tailored to your child's current reading level, he will need coaching on one out of every ten to twenty words. If he really doesn't need much help at all, it may be time to move to the next reading level. If your child needs help with every other word, you probably need to bump the reading level down by one half or a full level.

Basically, side-by-side reading is reading aloud with your child in a highly guided way. The important element is to help your child accurately decode each word by coaching him through the decoding when he needs help.

Whatever you do, don't get impatient or use an exasperated tone of voice. I know it's difficult when you just worked on the same sound in the previous word(s) or syllable(s), but if your child hasn't mastered the sound, he won't be able to recall it. Getting frustrated or angry won't help your child recall better—in fact, it is more likely to cause his brain to shut down. Therefore, calm, patient coaching is required.

Because your child must truly understand word structures and syllables to develop fluency with reading skills, this side-by-side practice will solidify the skills your child is learning in your Orton-Gillingham based program. Side-by-side reading can be very enjoyable when both parent and child are relaxed, so do your best to undertake side-by-side practice as a parent-child bonding time.

MULTISYLLABLE READING

Multi-syllable words are difficult for students with dyslexia to read. Perhaps the most difficult part is figuring out where to divide words in order to sound out each of the individual syllables.

Once your child has mastered basic reading skills and has completed most, if not all, of your Orton-Gillingham reading program, you may find your child still has difficulty decoding words with three or more syllables. While the comprehensive reading programs cover syllabication, most of the programs do not cover syllable division in sufficient depth for your child to gain mastery of division rules.

The O-G programs cover each of the syllable types and incorporate practice, but as with the basic skills, large amounts of practice are typically needed to provide your child with mastery and reading fluency. If your child struggles with multi-syllable words, you'll need to work through an advanced word-attack program.

In this chapter, I'll provide you with the names of some of the more popular and proven programs for developing word attack skills. The programs use various methods for segmenting, scooping syllables, drilling syllable rules, etc., so you'll want to look at the various programs' page samples to see which method will appeal to you and your child.

For the most part, word segmenting skills will be taught using workbooks and through side-by-side, guided reading techniques, which we covered in the prior chapter. Whether you use scooping, circles, or slashes to divide words won't matter in the long run as long as your child masters each of the syllable types–open, closed, unusual syllables like –sion and –tion, etc.

If your child is in public school and already has a lot of homework, you may want to wait until summer to use one of these multi-syllable instruction programs. It will be beneficial to wait until after your child has completed the computer-based practice programs you've chosen.

If you are homeschooling your child, then you can simply add one of these word skills programs to the language arts portion of your school day. As you complete your face-to-face, Orton-Gillingham program, it's natural to move right into one of these programs.

Learning advanced word-attack skills to the point of mastery will enable your child to read high school and college level texts, if he intends to go to college. When your child has mastered multisyllable word attack skills, he will be able to read just about anything he desires to read.

So, check out the programs that follow and pick one or two to use with your child. Some of the programs are much more robust than the others, so if you choose a program with eight levels (Megawords), you probably won't need to use a secondary program. If you choose a program that only has a couple of levels, the instruction may or may not be sufficient for your child to achieve mastery.

Additionally, if your child has a decent understanding of how to decode multisyllable words from the Orton-Gillingham program you used, then a program with a couple of levels might be completely sufficient. Just monitor your child's word attack abilities and adjust the level of instruction you provide accordingly.

You can have your child complete one or two pages in a workbook right before bed each night. Calibrate the amount of work your child does according to how fast he works.

Practicing word skills before bed is beneficial for the same reason I recommended using the computer-based practice program before bed—the instruction will be processed as your child goes to sleep, which helps with learning retention. For your consideration, here are some popular and successfully used advanced word attack programs:

Workbook-based Programs

Rewards Intermediate and Rewards Secondary - Rewards is one of the best and most liked advanced reading skills programs used by parents in the Learning Abled Kids' Support group. Rewards Intermediate and Secondary are for children who already read at a 2.5 grade level or higher at a minimum. Rewards is designed for 4th grade and higher. I would not recommend using it with a child in a lower grade because of the more advanced reading level of the words used in the lessons.

The Rewards program can provide notable advancements in students' ability to decode multi-syllable words over a relatively short instructional period. Using both the Intermediate and Secondary levels through to completion should give your child a good understanding of how to decipher multi-syllable words when reading.

The Rewards program levels are available for purchase from the publisher at:

http://store.cambiumlearning.com/rewards/.

Megawords – We used Megawords with our boys to solidify their advanced word reading skills. Megawords is also used by a large number of parents in the Learning Abled Kids' Support group and is well-liked for its thoroughness.

The Megawords program is very specific and sequential in teaching word attack skills. It has eight levels of instruction and each level adds a higher level of word attack skill. A level consists of a student workbook and a teacher's manual.

Working through each level took us about 1/2 to 2/3 of an academic year, so we worked through all eight levels in about three school years while homeschooling. The program was part of our typical language arts instruction each school day.

If your child is in a traditional school, it may take longer for your child to work through all eight levels of this program. Your child can complete a couple of pages during the weekend, and throughout holiday periods—especially summertime. Using the program regularly will provide steady forward progress. Megawords can be purchased through various book retailers.

Explode the Code Levels 4, 4½ and 8 – Explode the Code (ETC) is widely used for teaching children basic reading skills. The program is not specifically designed for remediation of dyslexia, but many parents of children with dyslexia use it for supplemental reading instruction. The program works well with children who have mild dyslexia (a lack of phonemic awareness only).

That said, Explode The Code can be used specifically to teach syllabication as a supplement to any Orton-Gillingham program. The three books in the ETC series which specifically teach syllables are books 4, 4½, and 8. Using these three ETC books will provide basic instruction in syllabication and some practice.

These three ETC books are recommended as a follow-up to your Orton-Gillingham program when your child needs additional instruction in syllabication using a different instructional approach. Many parents in the Learning Abled Kids' support group have found ETC to be an effective way to provide additional review and instruction when their children know the basic rules, but need more practice.

Given that Explode the Code is a very popular product, it can be purchased through most book retailers.

Direct Instruction Programs

The following three programs are parent-led. These programs are not workbook-based, so they require you to instruct your child directly.

Just Words (A Wilson Reading program) – This new program is designed for students who have mastery of basic reading skills but have difficulty with multisyllable words. Just Words is offered by the publishers of the long-proven Wilson Reading program.

Just Words is designed to move at an accelerated pace and is designed to last one academic year when used daily for about 45 minutes per day of direct instruction. This program is multi-sensory. Therefore, this program will be more interactive for your child, but that also means you need to have the ability to work well with your child to use Just Words effectively.

Sometimes, as a student gets older, he resists working with his mom or dad in the interest of being independent. If that is the case for your child, you might have more difficulty using Just Words effectively. I mention this because your child may be approaching high school when you reach the point in the dyslexia remediation process where syllable division is your main instructional focus.

Just Words is available for purchase at:

http://www.justwords.com/.

Advanced Language Toolkit – The Advanced Language Toolkit (ATK) is not a workbook-based program. It is similar to Just Words and is designed for you to work with your child in order to teach him advanced word attack skills. ATK assumes your child has already obtained a 6th grade reading ability.

ATK teaches advanced structures and organization within words. This program has 163 cards and teaches through parent-implemented multisensory practice.

Please note, this is not a scripted program. The Teacher's Manual explains how to use the kit and the order in which you will instruct your child, but it does not tell you what to do or say, or when to introduce new sounds. You will have to figure out what to say, when to say it, and set the pace of instruction yourself. However, this shouldn't be too difficult if you've already worked through a complete Orton-Gillingham program with your child.

While the marketing write-up says anyone can use this kit, even without Orton-Gillingham training, unless you understand the O-G methods, this program will be a bit more challenging to use than a workbook-based program.

I can speak from experience in using the Language Toolkit that having O-G training enabled me to use the program easily. Therefore, if you are uncertain about your O-G skills, you may want to buy and read The Gillingham Manual by Anna Gillingham.

As with Just Words, depending on how well you and your child work together or how much multisensory instruction helps your child, this program may or may not be your best choice. You can purchase the Advanced Language Toolkit through EPS at http://eps.schoolspecialty.com/.

Toe-by-Toe – This program is used in the U.K., and it is more unconventional than the other programs. However, parents sing its praises. Toe-by-Toe uses nonsense words for the bulk of the instruction, so the program works for any student who is learning the syllables in English words.

If you visit the website, you will see this is a simple, no bells or whistles type of program. There are no teacher's manuals—only student books—but the student books have teaching prompts in coaching boxes, so you will know what to do at each step along the way.

Toe-by-Toe is designed to be a full program solely for learning word divisions. It does not teach syllabication in the same way as many reading programs, but rather provides a lot of instruction and practice to the point of mastery.

Like Just Words and the Advanced Language Toolkit, Toe-by-Toe requires you to work one-on-one with your child. Therefore, it carries the same issues or concerns about your child's willingness to work with you as a major factor in whether this program will work well for your child.

The publisher says this program works very well for parents who approach the program with faith that it will teach syllable skills and who follow every instruction precisely. Those who come into the program wanting to skip parts, move ahead without mastery first, etc., will have poorer results, and I would add that would probably be the case with any of the programs used for remediating dyslexia.

As a quick recap, the workbook based programs are:

1) Megawords (provides the most comprehensive coverage),

2) Rewards (solid, well-liked program), and

3) Explode The Code books 4, 4 ½, and 8 (great for added instruction when a child needs skill reinforcement).

The programs requiring direct parental instruction are:

1) Just Words (a scripted program from the tried and true providers of Wilson Reading),

2) Advanced Language Toolkit (follow-up program to *The Language Toolkit* designed to work on advanced word studies), and

3) Toe-by-Toe (an unconventional, but thorough syllable instruction program from the U.K.)

It's really important for you to understand that reading fluency—being able to read easily without thinking too hard—is necessary for a child to be able to read and write at advanced levels. Writing is a much more complex skill than reading, so your child must develop good reading skills before good writing skills can be developed.

We'll talk more about the reason writing and spelling are very difficult for children with dyslexia in the next chapter. So let's now move into an entirely different challenge for children with dyslexia — WRITING!

THE ACT OF WRITING

It's important to note that your child must have good reading skills before good writing skills will emerge. That is because reading is based in recognition. Writing requires automatic memory and recall of the phonemes without providing your child anything to jar his memory.

The key difference is that reading places text right in front of your child, which he can look at and decode using the skills he's been taught for decoding words. Therefore, reading primarily requires recognition, with simpler recall of how to divide words and apply the sounds to the phonemes.

Conversely, writing provides no visual cue whatsoever for your child. Everything your child writes must be generated out of his own mind. Writing requires 100% recall of the sounds, syllables, spelling rules, etc.

The 100% required recall is why a lot of children are stymied by a blank piece of paper lying in front of them. With nothing to go on, their minds don't have a visual cue of where to begin.

Therefore, you must train your child to write using tools and techniques that will help him overcome the "blank page / blank mind" syndrome. We'll talk about the tools as we discuss each of the components of writing instruction.

There are two important skills your child must develop, aside from being able to read, in order to become a proficient writer. One is the mechanical or physical skill required in writing—or actually getting the words onto the paper. The other primary skill is called Written Expression, which is the skill of deciding what to write and how to express your thoughts on paper.

Your child must be able to use skills to get the physical words written on a paper and must be able to express himself. Although it would seem as if handwriting is required for a child to write, it is not actually a requirement for written compositions. A person can create written documents for school or for other purposes without putting his hand to paper by using assistive technology.

Handwriting is generally required to fill out forms, to sign paperwork, to write short notes to other people, etc. Therefore, handwriting is a skill that needs to be taught to your child, but it's important for you to separate your thinking about the need for good handwriting skills from any perception that handwriting is required to create a written document. Today's technology enables anyone to compose a document without the physical act of handwriting, much as I am dictating this book using Dragon NaturallySpeaking software.

To simplify the concept of handwriting separated from written expression, if your child can carry on conversations, explain to other people what he is thinking or doing, and otherwise express himself verbally, then he can create a written paper even if he hates handwriting.

Separating handwriting and written expression is key in helping children understand that they can be good writers even if they hate "writing." Generally speaking, kids hate handwriting more than they hate expressing themselves in a written form if the two skills are appropriately separated.

For example, both of my sons are excellent at writing compositions. Both of them earned A's in their dual enrollment English classes, but only one of them has "pretty" handwriting. In both cases, all of their compositions were presented in a typed format, so handwriting never came into the picture when written essays or papers were assigned.

So why do we torture children in grades K-12 by insisting they must write everything by hand? If you want to encourage your child's ability to express himself fluently when writing, then you can help a great deal by providing encouragement and assistive technology when the goal of the assignment is written expression.

The use of technology for writing is becoming increasingly acceptable in K-12 education. Hopefully, your child's school will begin using technology for written expression before your child reaches a point where he "hates" writing because it is physically difficult for him. Usually children hate writing by hand, but they don't hate expressing themselves in writing. Handwriting often becomes a roadblock for written expression.

In this chapter we will discuss handwriting and written expression as two totally separate aspects of writing. We will focus more on written expression because it is the primary goal of writing, and it can be accomplished without handwriting.

Nevertheless, handwriting is a necessary skill for life and, therefore, we must also be aware that handwriting should be taught until a child achieves handwriting that can be reasonably deciphered. Since handwriting usually comes first in a child's schooling we will address it first.

Handwriting

If your child does not have good fine motor dexterity, he will have difficulty with the physical act of writing. If your child also has dyslexia, figuring out what letters to use to write the desired words adds a layer of extreme difficulty to the task of writing by hand.

Many children with dyslexia also have deficits in their working memory, so it's very difficult for the child to hold a sentence he would like to write in his mind while he is figuring out the necessary letters to create the words in his sentence. If handwriting is labor-intensive for your child, there is a high likelihood he'll forget what he was trying to write even as he is in the process of writing.

Often, when writing by hand, a child with dyslexia will greatly simplify his sentences because the capacity of his working memory is limited. It's not that the child doesn't have sophisticated thoughts or ways of expressing himself, but trying to express himself in writing is an exhausting task. He simply does not have the functional working memory capacity to easily hold everything he is thinking in his mind while also figuring out the spelling of every single word.

Therefore, when working on handwriting with your child, I highly recommend using a dictation or copying approach. By separating the amount of working memory your child must use to write a sentence by hand from what is being written, you can help your child be more successful with the handwriting task.

For example, if you want your child to write, "The itsy-bitsy spider climbed up the water spout," you have a choice of telling your child the sentence word-by-word or you can provide him with the sentence already written so that he may copy the sentence to his own paper. Using dictation or copying allows your child to focus on his handwriting without the added stress of trying to hold everything in memory.

If you are working on stretching your child's working memory capacity, you can tell your child the entire sentence at once. Your child will need to remember the entire sentence as he is writing, which requires a lot of working memory power. Your child must try to sound out each word, recall from memory the letters that represent the phonemes in each word, and write each phoneme in the correct order to create each word. As he creates each word, he must remember the next word in the sentence, word by word, as he writes.

Thus, if you are trying to work on expanding your child's working memory in conjunction with his handwriting practice, you should be prepared to patiently repeat each sentence multiple times. Your child will probably drop words from his working memory as he's trying to figure out how to spell each word. Therefore, if you are using full-sentence dictation, you will have to repeat the sentence multiple times before your child successfully writes the sentence on paper.

Your awareness of just how difficult this task is for your child will go a long way in helping you remain patient with your child's learning struggles in this area. Needless to say, because of his dyslexia, your child will have difficulty with this task.

In the scenario of dictating slowly, word by word, your child will still have to hold the word in his mind as he recalls the phonemes necessary for writing and physically write the word on the paper. By slowing down the process and giving your child one word at a time, he is much more likely to be successful in writing each individual word.

I love to use this method, giving the child one word at a time without revealing the entire sentence. As your child writes each word, the sentence reveals itself. When your child has the entire sentence written, you can have him pause and read the sentence aloud. Often, a child is surprised by what he has been able to write. A high-five is always in order when he's written a lengthy or complex sentence!

If you use the copying method, your child does not have to hold any information in his working memory as he is practicing handwriting. Copying allows your child to singularly focus on the act of handwriting. Needless to say, that makes copying the best method to use when your child is beginning to learn how to write by hand. Once he knows how to form each letter, then you may want to move into single-word dictation followed by full-sentence dictation.

Given the complexity of brain processing required when a child has dyslexia, especially if he also has working memory deficits, I highly encourage you to use copying as your primary method when practicing handwriting. By separating the task of handwriting from unnecessary complexity, you will help your child develop the physical skill of writing by hand with less anxiety and difficulty.

There will come a day after your child has mastered the ability to write by hand and knows the phonemes, when he will be better equipped to write from his working memory. In the beginning though, if you focus solely on handwriting from a copying method, your child is far less likely to develop a hatred of handwriting or written expression.

In our discussion about handwriting, I'll share considerations for you, tools, and a couple of viable writing programs. Each program is offered with the assumption that you will work on handwriting as an isolated skill with your child in order to increase your child's likelihood of handwriting success.

When you begin working on handwriting with your child, if he has significant difficulty holding a pencil, positioning his hand, or expresses extreme fatigue while trying to write, you may want to consider taking your child for an occupational therapy (O/T) evaluation.

An occupational therapist can evaluate your child's fine motor skills and visual motor integration to determine whether your child needs therapy in order to effectively write by hand. Occupational therapy often includes hand exercises, using therapy putty, and practicing fine motor skills such as shoe tying, buttoning clothes, picking up small objects, and holding spoons, pencils, etc. It can be invaluable for enabling your child to write without the physical pain or discomfort that often accompanies poor fine motor control.

Having a proper pencil grip can also make a significant

difference in your child's ability to write smoothly or easily. When you have an occupational therapy evaluation, the therapist will make recommendations to you regarding special writing instruments or grips that can help your child properly hold a pencil.

If your child does not have any significant problem with fatigue, pain, or complaints about handwriting, then you may want to purchase simple rubber pencil grips to help position your child's fingers correctly around the pencil. Gummy rubber pencil grips provided a measurable level of comfort for my boys when they were learning to write by hand. Although my older son also had occupational therapy, the grips themselves helped ease his discomfort from his tight grip on the pencil.

If you'd like to try a pencil grip to see if it helps your child, you can go on Amazon and search for "pencil grips" and several types of grips will be displayed. We tried a couple of different types of grips, but the ergonomic grips that resemble the shape of a peanut were the grips that were the most comfortable to both of my boys. Your child may prefer a different type of grip, but I think the ergonomic grips are a great place to start.

Once your child is able to hold a pen or pencil properly, then he will be ready to start working on handwriting skills. Since handwriting is a fine motor skill which also requires eye-hand coordination, you can help develop your child's ability to use a pencil by encouraging him to solve maze puzzles, color, connect dots, and complete other puzzles.

While the main goal of handwriting is to be able to write words, the ability to hold and use a pencil can be built just as easily through games that seem more fun to a child than handwriting drills. Don't get me wrong, handwriting drills with letters are required, but the ability to use a pencil easily should be your first step in developing your child's skill foundation for handwriting.

I like to use maze puzzle books for their simplicity and

for the fun factor. To find good maze puzzle books, simply search on Amazon for "maze puzzle book." Look for books that are classified as easy when you are beginning to work on handwriting skills, and move up to medium difficulty mazes as your child is able to easily solve the easy puzzles.

You don't want to start with difficult puzzles because they will just frustrate your child, and that will make your child dislike the practice. Your goal is to teach the isolated skill of writing in the simplest way possible.

Another great tool, if your child knows number sequences and letter sequences, is to use connect-the-dots puzzle books. If your child is artistic, he may prefer drawing something. Like mazes, you'll want to begin with easy connect-the-dots drawings and move to the more complex ones as your child develops dexterity with the pencil. One of the benefits of using a connect-the-dots book is that it also helps your child practice numeric or alphabetic sequencing.

Connect-the-dots books usually only require drawing straight lines, so they are somewhat less desirable than mazes for writing practice. However, using both connect-the-dots books and maze books will provide some degree of variety in your child's pencil practice, which is likely to be more enjoyable for your child.

As your child develops the ability to write with a pencil, you can start using a handwriting program to practice writing letters and words. There are many programs on the market that you can use for handwriting development.

In the beginning, again for the sake of simplicity, try to pick a practice book or program that uses a simple lettering style. It is totally unnecessary to have fancy curlicues or elaborate lettering. While some artistic children may enjoy the fancy fonts in their writing, they can practice fancier lettering as their basic handwriting skills develop.

Here are a few handwriting programs that children with writing difficulties seem to prefer due to the simple, straightforward instruction as well as the simplistic lettering.

The programs are Explode the Code's "Get Ready," "Get Set," and "Go For The Code" series, "Handwriting Without Tears" (HWT) and the "Italic Handwriting Series" (IHS).

Explode the Code's set of preparation books includes three books: "Get Ready for The Code: Book A," "Get Set for The Code: Book B," and "Go for The Code: Book C." This series teaches the sounds of the consonants along with letter formation and basic phonemic awareness. The letter formations are initially practiced using a fingertip. These books are a good choice for introducing letter formation to a child who would benefit from the built-in focus on phonemic awareness.

"Handwriting Without Tears" is wonderful to use when you first begin working on lettering. HWT is multisensory, has writing guides, specialized paper that makes writing on lines easier, and straightforward instruction that is easy for you and your child to use. Many parents in the Learning Abled Kids' support group use HWT because it is one of the best programs you can choose for a child who struggles with handwriting.

After your child has finished the HWT program and/or the Explode the Code introduction series, he may still need additional writing practice. This is where I find the "Italic Handwriting Series" to be the next best step for handwriting practice. The IHS program is a step up from block print lettering, but the lettering style is not as complex as cursive writing.

Italic handwriting is a nice looking intermediate style for anyone. It allows your child's writing to look less like elementary school writing without requiring sophisticated pencil dexterity.

You may wonder, "Why is simplicity in handwriting important?" Whether or not your child has fine-motor or memory difficulties, your child's dyslexia will make writing by hand more difficult because of the extra processing needed to figure out how to spell each and every word.

Eliminate any concern about how to form letters when writing in order to help your child write more easily.

When your child has mastered handwriting either through HWT or IHS, or through both programs combined, then you can probably declare your child's handwriting "good enough." How good is good enough?

When your child has difficulty with writing, whether it is solely due to dyslexia or is diagnosable as dysgraphia also, you should set your handwriting standard to "legible." The only outcome that really matters in your child's life is whether other people can decipher your child's handwriting.

Think of it this way: how many doctors, other professionals, or members of your family have handwriting you can barely read—if you can read it at all? Beautiful handwriting is simply not required; legibility is advisable.

It's noteworthy to mention that our neuropsychologist helped me adopt legibility as an acceptable standard for handwriting. I was hoping for "easily readable," but after seven years of working on handwriting with my younger son, the doctor pointed out my son's visual-motor integration and combined neurological issues were not likely to bring about any additional improvement in his writing.

The doctor said he could decipher what my son had written and other people probably could too. Therefore, my son's handwriting was "good enough" for him to function in life. Working to make my son's writing effortless for others to read was not worth the stress my son felt when writing.

Much to my son's relief, his handwriting was declared "good enough" and we stopped working on improving his handwriting further. Our neuropsychologist was right. My son is now in college and his professors are able to decipher his handwriting well enough that the legibility has not been an issue.

As you are working on handwriting with your child, if your child begins to ask when you're going to be done working on handwriting forever, keep "good enough" in your mind as your completion standard. If your child's writing is reasonably legible, let his handwriting be as it is. No further handwriting practice is required.

When your child is learning lettering, you may find he likes using a Writing App on a touch-screen enabled tablet. There are several apps available which let children practice writing letters with their finger tip.

Although fingertip writing is not the same as handwriting, the finger tip writing on a tablet can help your child remember the shape of each letter. Your Orton-Gillingham based program will involve a lot of finger-tip writing, so you may not want a separate practice app for learning how to write the letters, but using a writing app on a tablet can add variety to your child's practice. Variety helps your child stay academically engaged while practicing.

Most notably, if you have an iPad, then you can get the app written by the Handwriting Without Tears publisher. The app is called, "Handwriting Without Tears: Wet-Dry-Try Suite for Capitals, Numbers & Lowercase." It's a mouthful, but worth checking out.

To find other appropriate practice apps, if you have an Android tablet, search in Amazon.com for "handwriting apps." If you have an iPad or iPod, you can find apps in the iTunes store by searching for "handwriting apps."

A Word about Keyboarding Skills

If your child has difficulty with handwriting, he may also have difficulty learning to type. However, learning to type is often easier for a child than the act of handwriting simply because typing is a less physically demanding skill than handwriting.

Whether or not your child ultimately outgrows his difficulties with handwriting, high school and college students are usually required to type their papers. Granted, your child can use the speech-to-text software to dictate his answers, but in the classroom environment, it is more difficult to use speech-to-text due to difficulties with background noise and/or the distraction that speaking causes for other students. Therefore, I highly recommend teaching your child keyboarding skills, whether his difficulties with writing are minor or significant.

Learning to keyboard requires practice. Difficulties with keyboarding usually stem from difficulty in remembering the letter locations. There are game-like software programs available to teach children how to type, and I highly recommend getting a fun program, then have your child practice regularly, so he will master the letter locations.

Keyboarding practice must take place daily for your child to make sufficient progress. Daily practice can be difficult to accomplish if your child is also working on learning to read, write, or spell. Since keyboarding is a great skill to have, but there are ways around it, I recommend saving daily keyboarding practice until after your child has finished his other remedial programs.

When you finish the other remedial programs, it may seem like your child no longer needs to learn keyboarding skills. However, writing by hand is likely to remain laborious for your child, so learning keyboarding can provide welcome relief from writing by hand. I'd urge you to help your child learn keyboarding as time permits.

If you're homeschooling your child, you may find learning to keyboard as a "subject" each day is an easy add-on. You'll just need to make sure your day is balanced and your child isn't overburdened with too much to do each day.

Written Expression

Whether or not your child has mastered handwriting, you can start teaching him to express himself in writing. You can make composition writing easy and interesting, particularly when you separate handwriting from the self-expression side of writing.

If your child has already learned to hate writing due to the practices used in his traditional program or because you were not aware of the benefit of separating handwriting from written expression, your task will be a bit tougher, but it is not impossible. If your child hates writing, then you may need to hit a reset button on your approach to writing. You'll want to focus solely on enabling your child to express himself in written form to help him get over any mental block he has developed in relation to writing.

For the remainder of this chapter, I will be focusing on written expression. Your child will need this skill to complete his K-12 schooling, but whether he needs it to any significant degree later in life will depend upon the career he chooses.

If your child intends to go to college, plans to become a business leader, or wants any other career that requires writing documents, he will definitely need to know how to express himself well in written form. Writing is the primary means for students to communicate what they know to their college professors. Business leaders often have to write emails or letters to others as a means of communication. Writing is essential in some careers but virtually unnecessary in others.

For example, if your child is more inclined toward becoming a plumber, HVAC technician, mechanic, home builder, etc., then he may never write another composition of any notable length in his lifetime. You'll need to weigh the depth of skill your child needs as you consider your remedial efforts in the area of writing.

If there is any chance your child will want to go into a career that will involve college or advanced studies, I'd urge you to consider developing your child's written expression abilities to the highest level he is capable of achieving. You do not want to sell your child's future short simply because written expression may be difficult to teach your child.

That said, let's look at some methods you may need to use if your child already "hates" writing. We'll follow these Reset Methods with insights about teaching your child advanced writing skills once he is willing to face writing with a mindset of creativity and self-expression.

Writing Reset Methods

If your child has already learned to hate writing by the time you're reading this book, then you may need to backpedal a bit in your writing instruction. In order to help your child overcome an instilled hatred for writing, one of the best things you can do is to reset by separating the physical act of writing by hand from the creation of compositions.

Your child can compose an essay without ever putting his hand to paper. There are two easy ways to accomplish this task.

The first way is for you to become your child's scribe. Your child can tell you what he would like to write in his essay or story, and you can write it down for him.

Some parents say, "But wait a minute! He needs to be able to write his own paper!" Parents are concerned about the child's ability to write his papers independently.

Independence will come. However, for a child with a significant learning disability in reading and writing, with writing being a very complex task, you'll need to help your child develop the ability to express himself in writing by taking one small step at a time.

One clever mom says she has her sons draw a picture

for any story she scribes for them. Illustrating their own stories gives her boys a fun way to practice the fine motor skills that are necessary for handwriting.

Also, having a scribe is a very common accommodation for students with significant writing disabilities. In colleges, students with disabilities are often assigned a note taker and are allowed to use computers for writing and taking tests. Having difficulty with the physical act of writing does not need to inhibit a child's ability to compose an essay.

Therefore, it is better to help your child learn to express himself in writing while you act as a scribe than it is to have writing be such a difficult task that your child doesn't want to do it at all. Once your child sees he can express himself well in writing, then you can help him find ways to independently get his words onto the paper.

The second method for separating the physical act of writing from the creation of an essay or story is to use dictation software. These days most computers have built-in speech-to-text capabilities. You can also buy high-quality software, such as Dragon NaturallySpeaking, to allow your child to "write" a paper by talking.

In other words, if your child can talk, then he can create an essay or story simply by talking into a microphone on his computer. Often this is the least intimidating way to show your child that he can create essays or stories easily. Using dictation software will show him that writing is simply putting whatever thoughts or ideas you have in your mind into written form.

A lot of children become intimidated when they're faced with a blank piece of paper and are expected to hand write a composition. Facing a blank computer screen can be similarly intimidating, but it is often easier for a child to start talking to his computer than it is for him to muster all of the processing required to write his thoughts on a piece of paper.

Not only is computer dictation less intimidating, kids often become fascinated with the dictation process. They love seeing what they say appear on the computer screen. Therefore, using speech-to-text software can make written expression seem fun.

If you're going to use dictation software, I will advise you that speech recognition capabilities vary widely from one program to another. Some programs accurately recognize what the speaker is saying, whereas others instill numerous text errors into the writing.

The introduction of dictation errors can be problematic for someone who is obsessively concerned about accuracy while dictating. However, if your child can be taught to simply talk and let the computer record what it hears, then you or your child can go back and correct mistakes within the text.

Sometimes it's difficult to decipher what you said at the time if the text is very poorly transcribed, but most of the time it's easy to remember what you said or meant to say. In the beginning, you may want to correct errors for your child as he tells you what he actually said, but as he gains skill with the phonemes, he can learn to correct the typos himself.

We prefer the Dragon NaturallySpeaking program because it has a dictation learning feature that helps the program learn how you express yourself as you use the program. Over time it becomes highly accurate at transcribing what you say into accurately formatted text.

It can be difficult for a child with a learning disability to train the Dragon NaturallySpeaking program because startup training requires reading passages on the computer. However, you can just start using the computer without reading the passages for training. Just be aware that starting from scratch without training will create more errors when your child first begins using the program.

These startup errors cause quite a few people to abandon the software before they ever get it trained. If you can calmly correct the initial dictation errors and know the software is learning from the corrections, then eventually the software will transcribe your child's dictation accurately.

Whether you decide to use your computer's built-in dictation software, a separately purchased voice recognition program, or you become your child's scribe, the next issue for you is likely to be what kind of writing curricula to use to teach your child writing skills at home. If you are helping your child reset his hatred of writing, then you will not want to jump into a heavy-duty composition program.

I would highly recommend starting with either daily journaling or the Brave Writer program. I don't know if there are other programs out there that are similar to Brave Writer, but we used Brave Writer when my boys were first brought home from public school. The Brave Writer program takes a conversational approach to writing and seeks to make writing easy by focusing on writing as a communication skill rather than an academic skill.

If you choose to use journaling, then you can simply have your child dictate to you (as a scribe), or dictate into his voice recognition software, his thoughts about any topic. You can have your child dictate his thoughts on his current science or social studies lessons, tell a story, or give his opinion about any number of topics.

The main goal with journaling or the Brave Writer program is to get your child to convey his thoughts in a conversational form, which are then put into a text format. When your child learns to see writing simply as expressing himself, just like he does in conversation, then composing an essay or story becomes much less intimidating. When my boys understood that writing is like talking to another person, but the words are written on paper, they were both able to move forward with learning how to write a well-structured essay or story.

Use journaling or Brave Writer for your writing instruction over a period of several months or an entire school year if your child hates writing and you are homeschooling your child. Using these methods over an extended period of time will help your child become genuinely comfortable with the conversational approach to written expression.

If your child is in public school and you are trying to help him overcome a hatred of writing, you should use dictation software with your child whenever you can to help him write any passages he needs to write for school. As an alternate approach, you can be your child's scribe while he is getting his initial thoughts on paper. After he has dictated the passage to you, then your child can practice handwriting by copying his dictated text onto the paper he will turn in for his assignment.

Let me stress here, do not write the paper for your child. If your child is in public school, not only is it cheating if you write the paper, it will also be detrimental to your child in the long run. It's just as detrimental if you're homeschooling. You will not help your child get over his difficulties with writing if you compose the paper for him.

I know a lot of parents think it's just easier for the parent to do the work and they don't want their child to fail. However, when your child creates his own written compositions, he will gain confidence and have more academic success in the future.

The big key, as was mentioned in the handwriting section, is to keep written expression separated from the physical act of putting the words on paper. As explained here, this task can be accomplished whether your child is in public school or homeschooled.

It's a little bit easier if your child is being homeschooled because these methods can be used throughout your child's school day. However, if your child is in public school, then it will be more difficult unless you can get your school to provide your child with appropriate accommodations using a scribe or dictation software during the school day.

Writing Compositions

Once your child is comfortable with putting words on paper through dictation, then you will need to help your child understand the structure of a good essay or story so that he can be successful in writing whatever he needs to write.

Tools which help a person see how to organize a paper include Graphic Organizers and mind mapping software such as Kidspiration or Inspiration. Using these tools will help a visual learner improve the structure of his essays, and the mind mapping software is effective for kinesthetic learners.

Graphic organizers come in a wide variety of formats for writing essays and for writing stories. You can easily find free, printable graphic organizers by searching on the Internet, and you can find books filled with graphic organizers on Amazon.com, Barnes and Noble, and in other bookstores.

Graphic organizers provide an outline or graphic format with prompts to help your child decide upon the topic for each paragraph of an essay or story. Detailed graphic organizers will help your child pick the main idea for each sentence within each paragraph in the essay.

Similarly you can find mind mapping software by searching on the Internet or on Amazon.com. Mind mapping software is a virtual type of graphic organizer with the basic difference being that the elements representing paragraphs or sentences can be reorganized by dragging them and dropping them in a different location. The mind mapping software allows your child to restructure his paper by dragging-and-dropping the sentences or paragraphs into a different order.

For example, if your child is writing a story about building a snowman, he might be excited about making the head, so he might initially say you should make a big snowball, stick a carrot nose in it, and place coal for eyes into the snowball. He may then talk about building the body and realize he's building his snowman upside down. The beauty of the mind mapping software is that he can simply select and drag the head-building paragraph down below the bodybuilding paragraphs and he doesn't have to rewrite anything.

It's easier to make structure changes in mind mapping software than it is to change the order of ideas in a graphic organizer. However, it is sometimes easier for a child to use a graphic organizer because the graphic organizer has prompts within it, a pre-organized structure, and often has numerically sequenced steps.

Mind mapping software requires a little bit higher level of functioning and understanding for a child to independently use. When starting a new document in a mind mapping program, the document is often blank to begin with, although you can import and use templates that are similar to using a graphic organizer.

Just be aware of the differences when choosing between using a graphic organizer or mind mapping software and choose whichever you believe will fit your child's needs best. A child who likes the computer would probably prefer the software, but the graphic organizers seem to be easier for most kids to use.

If you are acting as a scribe for your child, you can write each sentence on an index card or Post-it Note to allow your child to easily rearrange his story. Similarly, you can cut your child's story or outline into sentence strips for easy rearrangement.

Even if you use tools to help your child visualize the structure of his essays or stories, you may also need to help your child understand composition writing using a comprehensive writing program. Here again, if you are homeschooling your child, implementing a comprehensive writing program is easier because you can just incorporate it into your school day as part of your typical instruction.

For the sake of efficiency, you can have your child

write about topics he's learning in his other subjects. It's the same concept of learning efficiency we discussed in the section about choosing Hi/Lo books. There's no sense in having your child write solely for the sake of writing when you can reinforce his content-based learning through his written expression.

If your child is in public school, you probably won't be able to or want to add in a writing program during the traditional school year. However, you can easily use one of the following programs during the summer break in lieu of summer school. You would only have to use the program for an hour or so each day. Using the program daily throughout the summer will bring your child a better understanding of written composition by the end of the summer.

Parents of learning abled kids prefer the Student Writing Intensive (SWI) programs from the Institute for Excellence in Writing (IEW) or the program levels from Essentials in Writing (EIW) to help their children become skilled writers. You may find other great programs are available, but these two programs are currently the most well-liked for teaching Learning Abled Kids.

Both IEW's and EIW's programs are accompanied by teaching DVDs which kids love. The primary difference in the programs seems to be between the two presenters, Andrew Pudewa for IEW and Matthew Stephens for EIW. Different kids connect with one instructor or the other and there isn't really a good way for me to advise you in regard to which your child may prefer.

Both programs teach the fundamentals of writing using small, step-by-step instructions. The IEW program videos tend to be humorous and entertaining, but some of the terms used in the teaching seemed to go over the heads of some students.

For example, when adding adjectives to sentences they are called "dress-ups" in the IEW program because the adjectives are dressing up the sentence through description.

This concept seems to go over the heads of some kids. I've noticed this is more of a problem for younger children than it is for children in upper middle school or high school. Older students really seem to connect with Mr. Pudewa's sense of humor in relation to their dislike of writing.

Essentials in Writing (EIW) is preferred by those who need a very incremental approach to writing instruction, but the primary complaint about this program is that kids get bogged down in the details of the program. EIW is a more rigid and structured program than IEW, but the highly structured nature of the program is precisely what some children need.

I wish there were an easy way to tell you which of these programs would be best for your child, but it really is a matter of personal preference for your child. The best guidance I can offer is that if you have an older child, then IEW may be more relatable to your child, particularly if he has learned to dislike writing up to this point.

Writing Recap

To summarize, you'll want to keep the following considerations in mind when helping your child learn to write well:

1) Separate handwriting from written composition. This will help your child learn each of these skills as distinctly separate capabilities.

2) Begin teaching handwriting through copying in order to eliminate all of the mental effort that is required to compose words and sentences from scratch.

3) After your child has mastered the phonemes and mastered basic handwriting through copying, then you can introduce handwriting from dictation.

4)   Teaching your child keyboarding skills is beneficial whether or not he becomes proficient with writing by hand.

5)   Your child can express himself in writing, even before he has mastered handwriting, by using a scribe or dictation software.

6)   Begin teaching written composition to your child by using the concept of putting conversation onto paper.

7)   Use graphic organizers or mind mapping tools to help guide your child in the writing process.

8)   Use an audiovisual, step-by-step program to teach your child advanced writing skills for essays and stories.

Writing is a mentally draining task for most kids with dyslexia, particularly if the child has also been diagnosed with dysgraphia, working memory problems, or has a multi-dimensional form of dyslexia. Breaking up writing instruction into simplified steps of learning can help your child learn to write without feeling totally overwhelmed.

When your child learns to express himself in writing through small steps, you may be amazed at the creative writer that emerges from within. More often than not, when a learning abled kid is free to express himself through dictation, his fully creative, wonderfully imaginative self begins to emerge. Writing can become an avenue for great expression.

THE SPELLING NEMESIS

Ahh, the spelling nemesis. Spelling difficulties are highly resistant to remediation in children with severe phonemic awareness and working memory deficits. Spelling remediation can take place throughout a child's schooling, including through high school, and perfect spelling skills may never emerge. Overcoming persistent spelling struggles can seem impossible if your child has significant phonemic awareness deficits.

Does this mean your child will have to memorize weekly spelling lists for the entirety of his K-12 schooling? By no means! That would probably drive your child nuts, and he would most certainly hate working on spelling if he had to memorize spelling lists for 12+ years. Additionally, weekly spelling list memorization and testing has been proven to be an ineffective means for addressing the spelling difficulties caused by deficits in phonemic awareness.

Significant difficulty with spelling is evident in most children who have true dyslexia. Spelling correctly becomes even more complicated when a child has additional difficulties with working memory, recall or executive function deficits. If a child can't easily remember how to spell a word, or the various spellings of different homonyms, then he will often spell the words incorrectly.

As with reading instruction, it takes hundreds of repetitions before the correct spellings are easily used when writing. The good news is that a large portion of spelling instruction is covered within Orton-Gillingham based reading remediation programs.

If your child doesn't have severe spelling problems, using an Orton Gillingham reading program may be sufficient for teaching your child how to read and spell. This tends to be the case for children with mild dyslexia. For children with severe or multi-dimensional dyslexia, learning how to properly spell words takes an additional level of instruction that is provided in addition to Orton Gillingham reading instruction.

I will tell you that typical spelling lists for weekly spelling quizzes almost never work for a child with significant dyslexia. Your child may ace the test this week and correctly spell every word, but then later that day, or the next week, or whenever he next uses the words, your child will spell the word as if he's never learned to spell it at all.

Simply put, your child may not accurately remember how to spell each word without a lot of repetition. Even then it may seem like your child will never learn how to spell a word properly. Such was the case with my son and his spelling of the word "when."

Although we worked on the spelling of "when" for seven years, whenever he wrote the word, he always wrote "wen." Going into high school my son's spelling was still dreadful, although highly phonemic—he spelled everything exactly as it sounded. Since I was working on obtaining my Master's degree, as part of my program research, I began researching to learn, "What works for spelling?"

We'll get to the research in a minute, but first let's talk about how you can help your child learn rules for spelling, even if he is unable to apply them as he is writing. It's important for your child to learn the basic rules so that his words will be decipherable by readers even if his words are not spelled properly. Did you notice that word "decipherable" again? We used it in relation to handwriting, and you should know right away that decipherability is an applicable standard for spelling too—IF your child is not going to pursue a college education.

In this chapter, I will share with you the names of a few remedial spelling programs that are designed specifically for teaching children with dyslexia how to spell, and then I will share with you the research proven method for helping a child (usually a teen) overcome instruction-resistant spelling problems. Don't just skip ahead to the research proven method because, in order for that method to work, it is essential that your child has a foundational understanding of proper spelling first in order to use the method.

You may find that you will use a remedial spelling program and then need to move to the advanced spelling correction techniques. The degree to which you need to work on spelling will, of course, be dictated by your child's individual difficulties with spelling.

Remedial Spelling Programs

Whether or not your child is in a traditional school, you are highly likely to find traditional spelling tests bring about zero ability for your child to spell well. Many times a child in a traditional school will be subjected to weekly spelling tests, may even pass those tests, but then will fail to show any ability to spell well when writing.

It is critical for you to understand that isolated spelling of words for one test is entirely different from composing an entire sentence in one's brain, trying to hold the sentence in mind as he figures out how to spell each word, all while writing everything down on paper. Unless your child has memorized the spellings of every word in the sentence to the point of mastery, he is highly likely to have spelling errors in his sentence.

Teachers and parents may erroneously attribute the child's spelling errors to "laziness," because they fail to understand the complicated mental processes involved in trying to spell well. The inability to write and correctly spell every word is not laziness by any stretch. Spelling correctly while you are actively writing is a complicated mental process as we discussed in the previous chapter.

If your child is in traditional school, you may or may not be able to get your child's school to use the right kind of spelling program to help your child. If your child is in special education, they may use a program designed specifically to teach children with dyslexia how to spell.

However, if your child's school is not using the program properly or you see no meaningful progress in spelling, you may need to take matters into your own hands. As with everything else, if you are homeschooling your child, you will have an easier time implementing a spelling program as a part of your regular school day.

One thing is clear: if your child struggles tremendously with spelling, he needs spelling instruction designed for his kind of mind, and you might as well forget those weekly spelling tests.

The most commonly used remedial spelling programs for children with dyslexia are All About Spelling, Logic of English, The Phonetic Zoo, and AVKO Sequential Spelling.

All About Spelling – AAS is the most comprehensive, multisensory, explicit, direct instruction program in spelling that I have seen. It is designed specifically to teach spelling skills to children with language-based learning disabilities like dyslexia or auditory processing disorders.

The teaching methods in the program are based upon Orton-Gillingham methods. "All About Spelling" is a step-by-step program with scripting provided for the teaching parent, so you will understand how to use the program effectively.

"All About Spelling" starts by teaching the beginning skills required for spelling (and reading). Sound recognition and sound-symbol relationships are taught prior to attempting to teach word construction for spelling. "All About Spelling" has added emphasis on spelling rules because the program covers more than the recognition-recall needed for reading.

The levels in "All About Spelling" are laid out perfectly, with mastery of each step being heavily advised before moving on to the subsequent step. If you use this program as designed, and you ENSURE your child has achieved mastery of each step prior to moving to the next step, then it would be unlikely that your child would fail to make good progress with this program.

Mastery means your child knows the material well. You may be tempted to move ahead rather than spend time in repetitive review long enough to ensure your child's mastery because it is tedious to repeat the instruction as many times as is needed. It doesn't help your child to move ahead out of boredom though. It will help if you can find new, creative ways to practice using multisensory techniques.

As a step-by-step program, "All About Spelling" cannot be beat for both cost and quality. To me, it is also a viable substitute for more expensive, scripted reading programs such as Wilson and Barton.

Logic of English – LOE is an Orton-Gillingham based program that is comprehensive and multisensory. Parents find the program easy to use, and it provides a lot of great resources like a phonograms app, tactile handwriting cards, sandpaper letters, etc.

The biggest drawback for this program is that buying all of the elements of the program can be expensive. It is a great program, which Learning Abled Kids' parents really like, so it can be worth the cost.

Logic of English is heavily based upon research proven methods and practices. They have thoroughly documented the reasons behind different elements of their program and cited research as a foundation for their chosen methods.

That said, Logic of English is a relatively new program as of the writing of this book and does not (yet) have independent, scientific research studies documenting the effectiveness specifically of the LOE program itself. That's not to say it won't prove highly effective in a research study—in fact—I think it will be found to be effective when research has been done using this program.

I wanted to make you aware that LOE is based upon solid, research-proven practices but isn't yet proven as a stand alone program, in case that matters to you. If your child is in public school and you hope to get the school to use the program, they are required to use "proven" programs, so this one may not fill their bill yet. Check for the latest research to see if new studies specific to LOE have emerged.

The most important thing to me is that this program is solidly built upon Orton-Gillingham principles, is multisensory, and is effective for many Learning Abled Kids. Since it is easy for parents to use and they like it, I'm confident it's worth sharing as a viable option to consider.

The Phonetic Zoo – This program is published by the Institute for Excellence in Writing.

The Phonetic Zoo is not a beginner's spelling program. The words in the first level of The Phonetic Zoo are near a typical 4th grade level. The program assumes a child has an understanding of phonemes and basic spelling, so this program is a great follow-up program for either Megawords (discussed in the Multisyllable Reading chapter) or All About Spelling (listed above).

Most importantly, The Phonetic Zoo has a unique way of presenting and practicing words, which may be helpful for older spellers who have difficulty spelling. The publisher says, "When we look at a word we see it as a whole. But spelling is sequential, and the correct sequence can be missed when seen as a whole. Spelling the word out loud, letter by letter, ensures accurate storage of the correct sequence in the brain. Hence, auditory input is the best possible way to store spelling information accurately. The Phonetic Zoo combines phonetic spelling rules with the theme of animals and a zoo to illustrate the spelling rules."

The Phonetic Zoo program is primarily auditory in nature but it uses clever images and catchy phrases to provide your child with memory triggers.

The Phonetic Zoo comes in three levels. Each level uses the same spelling rules, but with more difficult words presented at the upper levels. The program moves toward more advanced spelling in small increments, which will help solidify your child's application of the spelling rules he already knows. I feel this program is best used to help your child with advanced spelling skills.

AVKO Sequential Spelling - This is a sequential spelling program based on multisensory teaching methods. It is a step-by-step program utilizing "word families" rather than phonemes. Many parents find this program easy to use and enjoyable for their child.

AVKO stands for "Auditory, Visual, Kinesthetic, and Oral." The program seeks to use each of these learning pathways in the instruction, so it is truly a multisensory program.

AVKO is a long-standing program that a lot of parents have tried. AVKO either works for a child or it doesn't. The word-families approach is different from most Orton-Gillingham based programs. O-G programs focus on rules and frequency of the rule application.

The word-families approach caused issues for my son, as it does for some other kids with dyslexia. When we worked on the "ate" sound—fate, rate, mate, plate, etc., my son did well with those words until we introduced "eight" as a word-family. Suddenly fate became feight, rate became reight, mate became meight, and plate became pleight! When writing, it was impossible for him to relate the word-family to the word he was currently writing.

In our case, my son's application of the word-family spellings always shifted as a different spelling for a same or similar sound was introduced. The word-family approach simply did not work well for my son.

AVKO does work for many children though, and it may be precisely what your child needs. It is a popular multisensory program, so it may work for your child.

Aside from the programs listed above, there are a number of spelling apps and programs online that you may find helpful when teaching your child to spell. You will find a more comprehensive, up-to-date listing of viable spelling programs at:

http://learningabledkids.com/language_arts/spelling.htm.

As always, feel free to search for newly published multisensory, Orton-Gillingham spelling programs and apps.

Research Proven Method for Spelling Correction

If your child has had YEARS of spelling instruction, but still has pervasive spelling difficulties, then you may be tempted to give up on your child's spelling instruction.

After I had remediated my son's reading issues due to dyslexia, and after working on spelling for years, he still had difficulty spelling basic words like who (ho), what (wat), when (wen), etc. Now my son spells excellently. Do you want to know our secret?

I embarked on a trail of research to figure out, "What works for spelling when all else fails?"

What Works for Pervasive Spelling Difficulties?

I read endless research findings seeking to discover what works for pervasive spelling errors. I wanted to know how to teach spelling to a child who has multi-dimensional dyslexia. The research clearly showed that correcting one's own spelling mistakes is one of the most effective, long-term means for improving spelling skills when a child has already been taught spelling rules.

Self-correction is not a method used in lieu of a formal spelling program, but it can be used after or in conjunction with a phonemic spelling program, like those listed in the first half of this chapter.

When a child with dyslexia or phonemic awareness deficits has had a formal spelling program, he may master the phonemes and spelling rules. Application, however, is a different issue. Even though he can recognize the proper spelling or recite spelling rules, your child may repeatedly apply the spelling rules incorrectly.

By self-correcting, your child will work on correcting the words he doesn't know how to spell on a repeated basis. Through repeated misspellings, and a desire to avoid correcting the same words repeatedly, a child will eventually remember the proper spellings better than he will with ongoing, standard spelling quizzes.

Simply put, self-correction is what works best for teaching a child to apply the spelling rules when he already knows the spelling rules. Self-correction teaches a child to pay close attention to spelling conventions and focus on the words he intends to spell as he writes.

How Does the Self-Correction Method Help a Child?

Although self-correcting is a relatively tedious process, it does the following:

1.   It inspires a child to recall the correct spelling more often when he is initially writing his composition, and

2.   It teaches valuable editing skills.

If you use self-correction, your child's spelling will improve over time, but it is a rather slow process. Self-correction is labor-intensive for your child, so you will want to begin with a reasonable level of self-correction. I recommend you start by having your child correct the first two sentences in a piece of writing, then move to the first paragraph as the child develops better self-correction skills.

When we started using the self-correction method, we began with a limited number of corrections, otherwise it might have taken half of a day for my son to correct all of his spelling errors. I didn't want to overwhelm him with the process, and you won't want to overwhelm your child either.

Begin by having your child correct a sentence or two. When your child has relatively few errors in his first few sentences, or can correct his errors quickly, then have him correct one or two paragraphs. After he's proficient with correcting a few paragraphs, have him correct a page, eventually moving toward correcting all errors in his whole paper. Alternately, you can start with self-correction of all three letter words, then four letter words, five letter words, and so on.

What is the Self-Correction Method?

Self-correction requires a couple of tools: A highlighter and a handheld phonemic speller. Here is how we used the self-correction process:

First, when my son would write a paper, I would simply highlight his spelling errors. You can see an example of how I highlighted his errors in the second-to-last sample on this webpage:

http://learningabledkids.com/learning_disability_ld/grade-by-grade-progress.htm).

On paper, you can use an ordinary highlighter to highlight your child's misspelled words. If your child is working in a word processor, I recommend using a word processor with spell checker enabled, so the program will highlight or underline all of the misspelled words.

Second, we bought our son a Franklin Speller to use when figuring out the correct spellings for words. A child with dyslexia needs this type of phonemic assistance in self-correcting because he often spells words quite differently than the actual spellings. However, he will usually spell the words with some degree of phonetic correctness.

With the Franklin Speller, your child can spell a word phonemically, like "sirip," and the Franklin Speller knows your child might mean "syrup" or "stirrup." The speller will display a list of words your child may have intended to spell.

The Franklin Speller will present multiple word choices. Your child can read the definitions provided through the Franklin Speller's dictionary function to see which word is the one he meant to spell. Your child can then correct the spelling for the word he intended to write.

Once your child has mastered the "process" of self-correcting using a Franklin Speller, it won't take as long for him to correct his own spelling mistakes. It takes quite a while the first several times because your child is figuring out how to use the Franklin Speller and may initially have difficulty with word recognition.

As you can see from this process, your child must have the ability to recognize the properly spelled word in order to effectively use a handheld speller. Franklin does have a talking speller, which we used initially, to help our son pick the proper word out of the list. Other brands of handheld spellers have features you may prefer, but we liked our first "talking" speller so well we bought a collegiate version for my son when he outgrew the talking speller.

While self-correction is a great method for helping a child master and apply correct spellings, you still need to work on explicit teaching of spelling before this method will work. Therefore, don't neglect direct instruction in spelling.

You can use the self-correction method when your child knows the rules and can tell you how to spell words correctly when he takes the time to think about spelling, but he routinely misspells the words when writing. Your child may still make a lot of spelling errors, but eventually he will become much more efficient at correcting them. If your child is like my son, self-correction will lead to excellent spelling in the long run.

READING AND WRITING ACCOMMODATIONS

Using assistive technology with your child prevents your child from missing out on content solely because he can't yet read or write. If your child cannot (yet) read, providing audiobooks, text-to-speech capability with content on computers, etc., for science, social studies, literature, and other subjects that are content-based just makes sense.

Therefore, I'm a firm believer in providing robust accommodations and assistive technology for content-area learning for any child who struggles. By using accommodations and assistive technology, your child can complete schoolwork at or near his actual academic aptitude.

The aim in providing robust accommodations using assistive technology is to avoid the "Matthew Effect," which is a phenomenon where children with disabilities in limited areas of educational skill (reading, writing, and math) tend to fall behind in ALL areas. Your child's disability affects history, science, literature, etc., when accommodations are not provided, even though your child is perfectly capable of understanding the concepts.

Although you put accommodations in place, your child will still need ongoing intense remediation in reading, writing, and math computation and other areas of disability he may have. If your child is receiving remedial instruction, accommodations will support your child until he gains the academic skills he needs in his areas of disability.

The goal of education is to prepare your child for his future, so accommodations should never be withheld based upon perceived "fairness," as many people argue. Accommodations should support your child in learning at or near his or her level of cognitive ability by eliminating barriers to learning that affect your child.

Each child deserves to learn as much as he can, by whatever means can be provided, so he can become as successful in life as possible. Why hold your child back from learning or meeting his potential? Don't let your child's school hold your child back by withholding accommodations either!

The difference between the "fairness" mindset and supporting a child at his or her own ability level is very important. Withholding accommodations can be particularly detrimental to children who are twice exceptional (gifted with learning disabilities) because they can understand content at a very high level and failing to provide needed accommodations can significantly hinder their conceptual understanding of content being taught. Again, why hold any child back from meeting his potential?

I would even argue that if your child is in public school and the school refuses to provide your child with accommodations to circumvent his area(s) of disability, then the school is withholding educational progress from your child. I consider the withholding of accommodations a form of educational neglect because it unnecessarily hinders a child's ability to learn. This is particularly true for content-based subjects like science, social studies, and literature.

Accommodations are tools to enable learning, not "crutches," as some people call them. While I don't like that analogy, ask yourself if you would withhold crutches or a wheelchair from a child who lost a leg because it would be unfair for that child to have assistance when no one else does? No—that would be ridiculous. Withholding tools for learning from a child with a learning disability is just as ridiculous, yet many schools routinely fail to provide meaningful accommodations to students with learning disabilities.

Some parents go along with the school's withholding of accommodations out of fear they'll "cripple" their child by using accommodations. In fact, the adults are hampering the child's learning by withholding necessary learning tools.

It isn't right to withhold accommodations because you or someone else is afraid your child may come to depend on the tools. Does a child who is missing a leg depend on his crutches throughout life?—You bet he does! Similarly, a learning disability needs tools to learn. Thus, your child should be taught to use assistive technology, so he can use it for learning and peak job performance throughout his life.

Don't let anyone talk you into withholding accommodations for your child based on misguided reasoning. Your goals are to be certain your child is progressing educationally, is learning at a level comparable to his cognitive abilities, and to equip your child with skills for peak performance throughout his life.

That said, let's talk about common accommodations for children who have dyslexia.

Reading Accommodations

Providing accommodations for reading difficulties keeps your child learning the same content as his peers. Even though your child may not be able to read, he still has the ability to learn about topics like dinosaurs, energy, world wars, great literature, etc. There is absolutely no reason whatsoever for your child to miss out on learning these types of academic topics.

The best way for your child to learn academic content while he is still learning to read is by reading books aloud to him, providing him with audiobooks, using text-to-speech software, or by using teaching videos/DVDs. There are many ways a child can learn about topics without reading books.

Let's look at the most common accommodations provided for students with reading disabilities.

Reading Aloud to Your Child

Sometimes the simplest accommodation is to read passages aloud to your child. This doesn't require any special technology or special formats, and your child doesn't have to learn to use a new tool. Anytime your child has content reading that is required for his schooling, he should have a read aloud accommodation until he reaches a point where he can read independently.

Having a "Reader" is an accommodation provided in colleges, on college entrance exams, and in some schools for kids who cannot yet read. The biggest hindrance to obtaining this accommodation is the availability of a person to act as a reader for your child. In the case of some public schools, the biggest hindrance is getting those schools to provide this accommodation on a regular basis.

If you're homeschooling your child, you can read anything and everything to your child. You will need to let your child do the reading when he's actually working on developing his reading skills, like during side-by-side reading practice discussed earlier in the book.

The biggest hindrance for homeschooling parents is usually the presence of siblings or an older child's unwillingness to have his mom (or dad) read his textbooks to him. In such cases, it's probably best to opt for the next type of accommodation—audiobooks.

Audiobooks

Audiobooks should be provided whenever content-based schoolwork requires reading and there is no one who is available to read aloud to your child. If your child's school does not provide a reader, they should always provide audiobooks for any educational content the students are required to read.

If your child is in public school, insist on a list of all the content-based books they will use during the school year for everything except reading decoding practice. Either you or the school should acquire the books in audio format for your child. Virtually all textbook publishers have audio versions of their books available these days, so the audio versions are generally fairly easy to obtain.

If your child is granted a reading accommodation in school, then your child's school should provide the audiobooks. If your child's school is being difficult, I'd highly recommend getting copies of the books for your child to use at home. Having audiobooks at home can cut down on homework time, improve your child's comprehension of the topic, and give him the opportunity to listen to the book content prior to being required to read it at school.

Providing audiobooks for pleasure reading can also help your child develop a love for reading. A child with a reading disability is unlikely to develop a love for books if his exposure to books is extremely limited because he can't read well. Consider getting most, if not all, of your child's books in audio format while he is still learning to read with the singular exception of books that will be used for reading decoding practice.

There are a number of places where you can find excellent audiobook recordings these days. Commercial providers include the iTunes Store, Audible.com, and LibriVox.org which offers public domain classics as free audiobooks. There are a number of Audio CD books available through Amazon.com also.

If have an evaluation documenting your child's reading disability, you can receive audiobooks through LearningAlly.org. They hold a vast collection of audio textbooks, literature classics, and audiobooks used by schools and colleges. There is an annual fee for this service, but it is well worth the cost if you use the audiobook service on an ongoing basis.

Text-to-Speech

If your child has content he must access on the Internet, using a tablet or via computer, you will want to check out the built-in text-to-speech functionality of the computer or other device. Most devices have built in text-to-speech functionality these days, so it is usually a matter of learning how to turn this feature on.

The text-to-speech feature is ideal when your child needs to do research using a computer but can't read the content of the webpage with the needed information. Your child can simply select the text, then have the device read the text aloud. The text-to-speech voices are usually digital, so it may take a little while before your child gets used to the robotic or mechanical nature of the voice.

We used Switched-On Schoolhouse's (SOS) learning programs for some of our academics because the software has a text-to-speech functionality built into it. When my boys encountered a word they didn't know, they could highlight the word and have it read aloud. This capability was helpful even though they could read fairly well before we started using SOS.

Educational DVDs

Children with dyslexia are frequently able to absorb and remember far more content when they watch educational TV or DVDs than they are able to remember when reading a book. That is because reading is such a labor intensive process, requiring so much brainwork, that the child forgets some of the content while he is working on decoding words.

You may find your child is able to remember all kinds of facts and information if he watches the History Channel, the Discovery Channel, or some other educational programming. If this is the case, consider the use of educational DVDs for any topic your child needs to study for his regular schoolwork.

Audio-visual learning can help your child learn, whether he is in public school or homeschooled. For example, if your child is studying the Gettysburg Address, you can watch a DVD about this famous speech. If he's learning about anatomy, watching a DVD about the human body makes it likely he will learn more than he would from his textbook.

While the information in a video will differ from your child's textbook, (unless the DVD and textbook are closely correlated), the content in the DVD program is likely to give your child a viable understanding of the topic. Additionally, hearing the terminology associated with images will help your child recognize the words more easily when he sees them in his textbook or on an exam.

For example, if your child encounters the word "cranium" while reading, he may have difficulty decoding the word. However, if he has heard the word, seen it in an audio-visual presentation, and knows it is related to the head, then he is more likely to be able to correctly decode the word when reading.

Watching videos alone, as they relate to classroom studies, may not be sufficient for passing nit-picky, fact-based tests at school, but the audio-visual programming will give your child a foundational understanding of the topic. Homeschooling parents can use audiovisual or DVD-based programs as their entire curriculum for any given subject.

For example, we used the History Channel's Classroom DVD set for our American History studies. We never had an American History textbook, but my son learned plenty from the series of DVDs. He learned enough to pass the U.S. History I and II CLEP exams and earn college credit— without ever reading a book about U.S. History.

All of the above are ways to accommodate your child's lack of reading skill until he is a proficient reader. You want to teach your child to read, and you'll be using a program to do that, but a lack of reading skill should not stand in the way of your child's ability to learn other topics.

You can find great Educational DVDs through Amazon.com, the Discovery Channel, the History Channel, National Geographic, and other educational entities. We checked out a large number of educational DVDs from our local library, so you may want to check your library to see if they have a DVD collection you can use as a resource.

Writing Accommodations

We talked about writing accommodations in the writing chapter, but I'll go into greater detail here. As we touched on in the writing chapter, children with written expression disabilities commonly write far less than they are capable of expressing orally when they are required to write by hand. A child with a writing disability will often use simple words he knows how to spell and are easy to write. Therefore, compositions seldom reflect the higher and deeper thoughts a child has about any given topic.

If you provide your child with assistive technology or other accommodations to allow her to dictate her stories and other compositions, your child is likely to compose stronger essays and greater stories. Assistive technology will enable your child to write at her cognitive level rather than being limited by her disabilities.

As mentioned earlier in the writing chapter, your child can use speech-to-text or a scribe for creating compositions about scientific, historical, or literary topics. She can dictate into a recorder or present her ideas orally to her teacher as other accommodated ways of expressing herself. There is no reason to prevent your child from expressing herself simply because her handwriting skills are slow and not (yet) developed.

While K-12 schools tend to be reluctant to provide a scribe or other reasonable writing accommodations, there is no reason to withhold this type of accommodation when the point of the written assignment is not to develop handwriting skills. In other words, if the point of the assignment is written expression, but your child has extreme difficulty with handwriting or the process of writing, then it just makes sense to provide an alternate means for your child to express himself or to transcribe his words onto paper.

Because K-12 schools are very reluctant to provide writing accommodations for a child, they impair the written expression development in children who have disabilities. If a child is provided accommodations, his writing can elevate to his level of cognitive ability and oral expression. No longer will compositions be limited to simple language nor will thoughts be withheld simply because they are too difficult for your child to express in written form.

To help your child develop the ability to express himself well in written form, your main goal is to enable your child to express his thoughts into a format that can be transcribed.

Speech-to-Text Software

As mentioned earlier, a lot of devices have built-in speech-to-text software. Dragon NaturallySpeaking is probably the most well-known dictation software package you can purchase, but there are many other dictation software packages available on the market.

Speech-to-text software can be very easy to use if the speech recognition is accurate. The accuracy varies widely between different types of apps and software packages. If the speech recognition is not of good quality, using a speech-to-text program can become a point of frustration for your child. Therefore, you'll want to buy the highest quality program you can reasonably afford.

Dictation programs require voice training in order to recognize the speech patterns of the person using the software. The period of time between when your software is brand-new and well-trained is a difficult phase because you will experience a lot of transcription errors in the beginning.

If your child is able to recognize the transcribing errors, and if he is a perfectionist, then the software training phase may be so frustrating for your child that he will refuse to use the software. This is where assistance and coaching can be of great benefit. You can encourage your child to dictate without becoming frustrated when re-speaking is required, and you can offer to correct all of the transcription errors for him until the program is reasonably well trained.

Once the software package is well trained, using the speech-to-text program for written expression becomes a breeze. It is so much easier for your child to speak his thoughts into a microphone than it is to write or type the words he wants to say.

As a writer with carpal tunnel syndrome, I use speech-to-text software regularly for dictation. From the voice of experience: If you can make it through the voice training phase, I think you and your child will agree that using voice recognition software for written expression is a true blessing.

Scribe

A scribe is simply someone who writes down whatever a student says. The scribe does not alter what the student says in any way, but simply puts the child's words onto the paper in written form.

If you are going to act as your child's scribe, it's essential for you to separate your own thoughts about what is being written from what your child actually says. A scribe simply puts the child's words onto the paper exactly as spoken, so the writing is fully the creation of the speaker.

It is important for your child's words to be recorded verbatim, so your child's words can be read back to him and he will learn how he sounds when expressing himself. By hearing his own words, he will be encouraged to change his self-expression to better fit what he intends to say.

Having a scribe or a note taker is a common accommodation in college for students with learning disabilities. This includes students with well-documented dyslexia, dysgraphia, and even attention deficit disorders.

Having a scribe requires an additional person's time. As such, I think the main reason K-12 schools are reluctant to provide a scribe is because of the difficulty they perceive with having someone act as a scribe for your child. While it is sometimes difficult for a school to provide a scribe, the difficulty does not excuse the school from their obligation to provide your child with a scribe or an accommodated means for written expression development given a disability in the area of handwriting.

There are creative solutions available if the adults put their heads together and consider all available resources. For example, in some cases I have known schools that have allowed the parents to become a scribe for their child during school hours. Often the scribe is the mom. Sometimes the family can afford to hire an assistant for the child, who becomes the child's scribe. At other times, a student who finishes her own work quickly will welcome the opportunity to scribe for your child in exchange for volunteer credit hours (which are often held in high value by kids applying to colleges).

I know a couple of school districts where the high school is directly across the street from or adjacent to the elementary school. High school students who want a teacher-based work study walk over to the elementary school for a select number of periods each week. Those high school students act as scribes or otherwise assist elementary children with disabilities in writing and spelling. Again, this can be done for work-study credit or volunteer credit hours. Either way, it is a win-win situation when schools use this innovative approach.

While it is the school district's responsibility to provide and pay for a scribe under IDEA, if the district refuses to provide a scribe or can't afford to provide one, for the sake of your child, I recommend trying to work out a creative solution with the school. It's better to provide what your child needs than to let your child suffer while quibbling over whose responsibility it is to provide the services.

If you are homeschooling, you are free to use this accommodation at will. You can easily act as your child's scribe anytime a scribe is needed.

The need for a scribe in elementary school is usually a temporary accommodation that is only needed until your child masters writing by hand. If difficulties with writing continue into high school, it's best to train your child to use a keyboard, dictation software, or other technologies in order to minimize the requirement for a scribe as the child moves to higher levels of education. Scribes are often, but not always, available.

Regardless of whether your child needs a scribe or not, always keep in mind that expressing oneself in written form, a.k.a. written expression, is a distinctly different skill from handwriting. Therefore, providing a scribe or speech-to-text software is a reasonable accommodation for anyone who has ongoing difficulty with written expression due to difficulty with writing by hand.

Note Taking

If your child is in school, you should also know there are two viable solutions for note-taking. The first is the use of carbonless notepaper which is available at office or school supply stores as well as on Amazon. To use the duplicate paper method, another student who is adept at taking notes simply uses the duplicate paper to take her own notes. At the end of class, the note taking student hands the duplicate copy of the notes to your child.

If your child wants to remain anonymous as the recipient of the notes, a pass-off system is often implemented. The note taker gives the second copy of the notes to the teacher. The teacher passes the notes on to your child directly or through a teacher who has your child in her class later in the day.

The second option is for the teacher to give your child a printed copy of the required notes. Teachers generally copy their own teaching notes and hand out copies to the students who need a copy. Neither of these options require an additional person, so they are easy accommodations to implement.

Dictation

Dictation may seem to be the same thing as having a scribe, but in the case of dictation, your child's words are usually left in oral form on a recording device. In order to use dictation as an accommodation, your child will need a voice recorder, usually a digital recorder.

When your child needs to "write" an answer, he simply dictates his answers into the voice recorder. The recorded response from the student is turned in as his final product.

Using dictation can be difficult because your child cannot easily modify or re-speak sentences he'd like to change. The inability to easily modify dictated answers is not a problem for short-answer questions, but it can be a significant issue if your child is creating a lengthier composition, like an essay or a story.

Thus, dictation is often a viable way for your child to answer questions on tests or worksheets where sharing his knowledge is the primary goal of the assignment. For example, if your child has biology homework and he has a worksheet where he must define several terms and give short explanations for biological processes, your child can dictate his answers into a recording device.

The typical format for worksheet dictation is for the child to state the name of the worksheet, the student's name, then "question one" followed by the answer to question #1, then "question two" followed by the answer to question #2, etc. If your child changes his mind about an answer, he can say, "Strike that last response to question #2 and change my answer to ___."

When grading the student's work, the teacher simply listens to the student responses and usually records the grade and commentary on a blank worksheet. The teacher returns the graded worksheet and the recording to the student at the same time she hands the rest of the class's papers back.

Using dictation for homework can significantly cut down on the time required for your child to complete his homework when handwriting is laborious for him. Using dictation is easy on both your child and his teacher once they both become accustomed to using dictated answers.

If you're homeschooling, you probably don't need to use dictation as you can use "Oral Communication," as presented in the next accommodation bullet. However, as your child gets older, he may prefer dictation as a way of working independently. Also, if you have other children you are homeschooling, then dictation can free up your availability to work with all of your children and you can listen to the dictated answers as time permits.

Oral Communication

While "Oral Communication" is very similar to dictation, it is a direct means for your child to answer questions or convey his thoughts to you or his teacher. Oral communication is simply using spoken responses instead of written responses, whether for worksheets, testing, or discussion to determine if your child understands the topic.

To use an oral communication accommodation, the teacher simply asks your child the questions directly, and your child answers directly. There is no intermediate recording or writing of your child's responses, although your child's teacher may choose to write down his responses for record-keeping purposes.

When the point of any assignment is to determine if your child understands the topic being studied, having a conversation with the teacher about the topic is a natural and viable way for the teacher to determine what your child knows. The difficulty with letting your child respond orally is that your child's teacher may find it difficult to receive oral responses from your child on every occasion. Similar to having a scribe, using oral communication requires a dedicated person to listen to your child's oral responses, whether that person is a teacher, you, or someone else.

If your child has a study period during the day, or his teacher has time before or after class, your child's teacher may find oral communication is easiest for discerning your child's level of learning.

I've found that using oral communication is the quickest and easiest accommodation to use. However, it is also the hardest to implement as a primary accommodation in a traditional school setting given the time required by both teacher and student.

Thus, oral communication is usually best used as one of several different ways your child may be permitted to respond without writing his answers. If your child's teacher has the time and ability to discuss answers with your child, then oral communication may be used.

It's a good idea to have alternate accommodations established for written responses. Having accommodations that permit responses by oral communication, dictation, a scribe, or speech-to-text works best because your child can respond according to the most effective way of responding in each individual class or situation.

If you're homeschooling and you don't have other children who need your attention too, then simply discussing answers with your child will be your easiest way to determine whether your child understands the concepts he is learning. Oral communication is just a simple extension of your regular teaching and discussion with your child.

Math Accommodations

Memorization of math facts is difficult for many people and is typically an issue for children with poor memory-recall functioning. Given that memory functioning is frequently an issue for children with multi-dimensional dyslexia, it is not unusual for a child with dyslexia to have difficulty working with math facts. Not only do many students who have dyslexia also have difficulty with math facts, it is difficult for them to read and understand the problems or to use their working memory to keep math facts straight as they solve a problem.

Similar to difficulties with reading and writing skills, the inability to remember math facts should not be a barrier to further math education. Accommodations can help your child with math difficulties stemming from his dyslexia.

For math, there are professionals on both sides of the

calculator versus no calculator argument. However, as one person who had trouble doing math in his head said to me, "That's what calculators are for."

Using a calculator for math is very similar to the need to separate the act of handwriting from written expression. Using a calculator separates the memory/recall aspect of math facts from the application of math concepts.

If your child hasn't been able to memorize math facts, he can still learn math concepts when he's permitted to use a calculator. If your child understands the application of higher level math concepts, it really makes no sense to prevent him from learning the math concepts simply because he can't remember math facts.

That said, if your child struggles with the memory and recall of his math facts, there are math programs designed for practicing math facts. You may need to have your child practice with one of these programs so he can improve his math fact fluency.

Reflex Math is one of the best program most loved by Learning Abled Kids' parents as a means of helping their children master math facts. There are other math practice programs listed at:

http://learningabledkids.com/multi_sensory_training/free-multisensory-curriculum-online.htm.

If your child struggles significantly with math, you may want to consider using one of the math programs listed at:

http://learningabledkids.com/mathematics/mathematics.htm.

Research the learning disability called dyscalculia too. It is similar to dyslexia and requires a similar protocol for teaching math skills as diagnosable dyslexia requires for the development of reading skills. You can find more information about dyscalculia on the Learning Abled Kids' website.

REVIEW AND SUMMARY

This chapter is designed to give you a handy, all-in-one, step-by-step reference list to use when addressing your child's dyslexia-based learning disabilities. The following items are presented in the order of recommended provisioning with physical needs addressed prior to, or in conjunction with, cognitive and learning needs:

1) Dyslexia by Definition as a Physical or Cognitive barrier to Reading:

☐ Scotopic Sensitivity or Irlen Syndrome (Corrected through colored glasses or overlays, lighting adjustments, colored papers, etc., Irlen Institute.)

☐ Ocular Motor Deficiencies (Corrected through COVD Vision Therapy)

☐ Visual-Perception Deficits (Corrected through Davis Method, Mind's Eye, or other visual-perception programs.)

☐ Auditory Processing Disorder (Corrected through Fast ForWord, The Listening Program, Linguisystems, or by a Speech-Language Therapist.)

☐ Cognitive Function Enhancement (Programs for memory, processing speed, Attention Deficit. Hyperactivity Disorder (ADHD), etc.)

2) Dyslexia by Diagnosis: A lack of phonemic awareness with or without additional physical or cognitive deficits. Diagnosis requires a comprehensive evaluation to assess your child's complete neurological learning profile.

- **Simple, Vanilla Dyslexia** – Lacking phonemic awareness without other cognitive function deficits.

- **Stealth Dyslexia** – Lacking phonemic awareness with intellectual giftedness, usually resulting in writing difficulties and delayed discovery of the underlying dyslexia.

- **Double Deficient Dyslexia** – Lacking phonemic awareness in addition to neurological processing speed deficits.

- **Multi-Dimensional Dyslexia** – Lacking phonemic awareness with additional deficits in processing, perception, comprehension, executive functioning, attention, or any number of other conditions that impair traditional classroom learning.

3) Addressing Public School Issues

- Participate in a Classroom Observation

- Research Your School's Track Record

- Develop Advocacy Skills

4) Training You May Need to Teach Your Child

- Multisensory Teaching Techniques

- The Orton-Gillingham methodology

A Review of Reading Instruction Practice Protocols

1) If your child has severe phonemic awareness problems, begin with one of the Phonemic Awareness Programs. Provide both face-to-face instruction and computer-based practice until your child masters the basic phonemes.

2) When your child has mastered the basic phonemes, then you can proceed with a traditional Orton-Gillingham program and a computer-based practice on a daily basis.

3) Begin guided reading practice as part of your evening routine (reading together) when your child is able to decode simple one or two syllable words.

5) Phonemic Awareness Instruction for Significant Phonemic Awareness Deficits and Speech-language Difficulties:

☐ Lindamood-Bell LiPS

☐ Fast Forword® and BrainPro®

Computer Programs for Phonemic Awareness Practice:

☐ Language Tune-Up Kit (LTK)

☐ Sound Reading

☐ Earobics

☐ Hear Builder Phonological Awareness

6) Do-It-Yourself Orton-Gillingham Programs for Remediating Deficiencies in Phonemic Awareness:

- ☐ ABeCeDanarian
- ☐ All About Reading
- ☐ Barton Reading And Spelling System
- ☐ New Herman Method, The
- ☐ S.P.I.R.E.
- ☐ Wilson Reading System

Orton-Gillingham Optional App:

- ☐ SoundLiteracy by 3D Literacy, LLC.

7) Comprehensive Reading Skills Practice Programs to Use in Conjunction With an Orton-Gillingham Program:

- ☐ Lexia Reading (http://lexialearning.com/)
- ☐ Language Tune-Up Kit (http://www.jwor.com)

Beginning Skills Practice Programs to be followed by a more advanced program:

- ☐ Funnix Reading (http://funnix.com/)
- ☐ Reading Eggs (http://readingeggs.com/)
- ☐ Earobics
- ☐ Simon Sounds it Out

Practice Apps for Android Devices

- ☐ Doodling Dragons by Pedia Learning Inc.
- ☐ Montessori Words & Phonics for Kids by L'Escapadou

Practice Apps for iPad <u>or</u> iPod (Apple)

- ☐ Phonics With Phonograms by Logic of English
- ☐ abc PocketPhonics: letter sounds & writing + first words by My Pocket Ltd
- ☐ OG Card Deck by Mayerson Academy
- ☐ Simplex Spelling Phonics - Rhyming With CVC Words by Pyxwise Software Inc.

Practice Apps for iPad (Apple)

- ☐ Learn to Read, Write and Spell by Rogers Center for Learning
- ☐ SoundLiteracy by 3D Literacy, LLC

8) Multisyllable Reading

Workbook-based Programs

- ☐ Rewards Intermediate and Rewards Secondary
- ☐ Megawords
- ☐ Explode the Code Levels 4, 4.5 and 8

Direct Instruction Programs

- ☐ Just Words
- ☐ Advanced Language Toolkit
- ☐ Toe-by-Toe

9) Side-by-Side Guided Reading Practice

Specialty Hi-Lo Book Publishers

- ☐ Amazon.com
- ☐ Wieser Educational Resources
- ☐ Bearport Publishing
- ☐ Bright Apple
- ☐ Capstone Classroom
- ☐ High Noon Books
- ☐ Perfection Learning
- ☐ Pro•ed
- ☐ Remedia Publications
- ☐ Sundance Publishing

Side-by-Side Reading Tools

- ☐ Index card or Guided Reading Strips
- ☐ Pencil, pen, or pointing implement

A Review of Writing Instruction Practice Protocols:

1) Separate handwriting from written composition.

2) Begin teaching handwriting through copying.

3) When your child has mastered basic handwriting skills and the phonemes, introduce dictation.

4) Begin teaching written composition to your child by using the concept of putting conversation onto paper.

5) Use graphic organizers or mind mapping tools.

6) Use a scribe or dictation software for essays or stories.

7) Use an audiovisual, step-by-step writing program

10) Handwriting

☐ Occupational therapy (O/T) evaluation

☐ Pencil grips

☐ Maze puzzles, coloring, connect the dots, and other puzzles

☐ Copying

☐ Dictation

Handwriting Programs

☐ "Handwriting Without Tears" (HWT)

☐ "Italic Handwriting Series" (IHS)

Writing Practice App - "Handwriting Without Tears: Wet-Dry-Try Suite for Capitals, Numbers & Lowercase."

11) Written Expression

Writing Reset Methods

- ☐ Brave Writer
- ☐ Scribe
- ☐ Journaling

Writing Composition Tools

- ☐ Graphic Organizers
- ☐ Mind mapping software
- ☐ Kidspiration
- ☐ Inspiration
- ☐ Keyboarding skills

Comprehensive Writing Composition Programs

- ☐ Institute for Excellence in Writing (IEW)
- ☐ Essentials in Writing (EIW)

12) Spelling

Remedial Spelling Programs

- ☐ All About Spelling
- ☐ Logic of English
- ☐ The Phonetic Zoo
- ☐ AVKO Sequential Spelling

Self-Correction for Spelling

Tools:

- ☐ A highlighter
- ☐ Handheld phonemic speller

12) Accommodations

Reading Accommodations

- ☐ Read Aloud
- ☐ Audiobooks
- ☐ Text-to-Speech
- ☐ Educational Videos/DVDs

Writing Accommodations

- ☐ Speech-to-Text software
- ☐ Scribe
- ☐ Note Taking
- ☐ Dictation
- ☐ Oral Communication
- ☐ Keyboarding Skills

Math Accommodations

- ☐ Calculator
- ☐ Reflex Math
- ☐ Math Practice Programs Listed at:
http://learningabledkids.com/multi_sensory_training/free-multisensory-curriculum-online.htm

If you are homeschooling your child, depending on your state requirements, you will want to focus on your child's core academic skills first and foremost. Use the summary checklists above as a means of designing a remedial reading and writing program for your child.

To design a viable program, be sure your child's program includes the following elements:

1) Therapies as needed for vision, reading or writing,

2) Remedial reading instruction geared directly toward your child's needs with both direct instruction and computer-based practice,

3) A spelling program geared toward your child's needs,

4) A handwriting program if needed,

5) A written expression program if needed,

6) And keyboarding if time permits.

Your state may also require science, social studies, or other subjects to be taught on a daily basis. If that is the case, consider using carefully selected, non-fiction Hi-Lo books for your child's reading practice. Focus on selecting non-fiction topics for required subjects for your child's written expression assignments.

By focusing your child's reading and written expression practice on the required subjects, you can build learning efficiency into your child's educational day, which will leave valuable time for esteem-building, extra-curricular activities. Every child needs to have time for fun and/or to participate in activities he loves and can excel in.

If your child is in a traditional school, I'm assuming his educational provisioning is not awesome, or you wouldn't be reading this book. In such a case, you need to arm yourself with strong knowledge about your child's educational rights. Learn how to be an effective advocate for your child so you can ensure your child makes meaningful educational progress through programs that actually meet his individual needs.

Wrightslaw.com and FETAweb.org are the two best websites I know for arming yourself with the information you need to become a strong and effective advocate for your child. If your child's school is not meeting his needs, these sites can help you learn how to get what your child needs.

If your child is not being schooled by you and you are not in control of your child's education, you will face challenges in getting the educational help your child needs. Since you are not in control of your child's education, you are—to a degree—at the mercy of your child's school.

There are some great districts out there, so I pray you are lucky enough to live in a great district, but I suspect not if you are reading this book! If your child's school is providing excellent services for your child, but you want to see more in the way of academic progress, then focus your efforts at home on practice, practice, practice followed by advanced reading and writing skill building. The additional instructional practice before bed, and additional remedial instruction during the summer, can make a significant difference in your child's academic progress.

The degree of difficulty you have in obtaining the help your child needs through your school district will totally depend upon your school district's mindset toward serving students with disabilities. Many districts let kids fall through the cracks or fight against parents over the provision of services to a child.

If your child's school is dragging their feet in providing services, resisting providing accommodations, or writes services into your child's IEP but fails to follow the IEP, then for the sake of your child, you need to do something. You either have to fight the school through due process avenues to get them to provide a proper education, or you need to provide what your child needs independently.

Often, providing what your child needs independently is

the path of least resistance. The cost can balance out no matter which route you take because getting a lawyer to force a resistant school to help your child is expensive.

What you can't afford is to let your child flounder educationally so that he ends up failing or dropping out of school before earning a diploma. Providing the therapies and programs your child needs is expensive, but at least you know your child is getting the help he needs.

If your child's school is difficult to work with, please do consider taking total control of your child's education for a period of two to three years. While homeschooling is not possible for some families, if you can find a way to homeschool even for a little while, it is well worth your time to make sure your child becomes successful academically.

Do not let your fears about homeschooling scare you away from providing the education your child needs. Read *"Overcome Your Fear of Homeschooling"* before you discard homeschooling as an option. It could make the difference in providing a viable educational outcome for your child and the utter destruction of your child. Trust me, homeschooling is a lot easier than you'd think because your entire household and family dynamics can change for the better when you bring your child home to learn.

My goal is to help every parent provide her child with the education every child deserves. If you have any questions or concerns, feel free to contact me through my website: http://learningabledkids.com contact information. I'll be happy to try to point you toward resources that may help you provide your child with a fabulous educational outcome. You can teach your child to read! I did it—You can too!

If you've found this book helpful, please leave a quick review on Amazon to let other parents know how this book can help them meet their children's needs. I value your input. I truly appreciate your focus on helping your child as well as encouraging other parents. Many Blessings to you!

REFERENCES

Eide Neurolearning Blog, (2013). Reference Accessed
December 2013.
http://eideneurolearningblog.blogspot.com/2005/09/stea
lth-dyslexia-when-writing-is.html

International Dyslexia Association, (2013). Reference
accessed November 2013:
http://www.interdys.org/FAQWhatIs.htm

National Institute of Neurological Disorders and Stroke,
(2013). Reference accessed November 2013:
http://www.ninds.nih.gov/disorders/dyslexia/dyslexia.ht
m

Torgesen, J. K., et al., (2010). Computer-assisted instruction
to prevent early reading difficulties in students at risk
for dyslexia: Outcomes from two instructional
approaches. Annals of Dyslexia. Vol 60, Issue 1.

ABOUT THE AUTHOR

Sandra K. Cook, a.k.a. Sandy, is a veteran home-schooling mom of boys with unique learning needs and the founder of Learning Abled Kids, L.L.C.

While homeschooling, Sandy earned her Master's Degree in Instructional Design and graduated Summa Cum Laude. She focused on Universal Design for Learning, Learning Styles, and Multisensory Instruction during her Master's Degree studies.

Sandy has also completed comprehensive Orton-Gillingham training, Georgia Advocacy Office's Parent Leadership Advocacy training, Georgia Charter School Association's "Organization and Concept Development" Training, is a Petitioner for American Sign Language for Georgia Students, and is a Lifetime Member of Phi Kappa Phi Academic Honor Society.

Sandy provides resources, information, and support for parents homeschooling children with learning disabilities through an online support group with well over 1500 members. She also provides information and resources through her website http://LearningAbledKids.com.

Sandy is also the author of:

Overcome Your Fear of Homeschooling,

How To Homeschool Your Learning Abled Kid: 75 Questions Answered,

Reading Comprehension for Kids, and

Cook's Prize Winning Annual Meal Planning System,

which are available on Amazon.com.

Recreationally, Sandy enjoys spending time with her husband and sons, walking with God, photography, bowling, kayaking, and lifelong learning.

SANDRA K. COOK